T0307579

MILITARY PRISONS
OF THE
CIVIL WAR

LIBBY PRISON, RICHMOND, VA.

MILITARY PRISONS
OF THE
CIVIL WAR

A COMPARATIVE STUDY

DAVID L. KELLER

WESTHOLME
Yardley

To Russell L. Lewis, Jr. (1951-2019), Executive Vice President and Chief Historian, Chicago History Museum. A great friend and mentor.

©2021 David L. Keller
Map by Tracy Dungan
Map © 2021 Westholme Publishing

Westholme Publishing, LLC
904 Edgewood Road
Yardley, Pennsylvania 19067
Visit our Web site at www.westholmepublishing.com

ISBN: 978-1-59416-357-9
Also available as an eBook.

Printed in the United States of America.

"A prisoner of war is a man who tries to kill you and fails and then asks you not to kill him."

—Winston Churchill, *Observer*, 1952

"Wars produce many stories of fiction, some of which are told until they are believed to be true."

—Ulysses S. Grant

CONTENTS

Illustrations

FOREWORD

By some counts, there have been eighty thousand books written on the Civil War, about ten books a week every week since Appomattox. So what is left to research and write about? Some of those books have been written about prisoners of war and the camps in which they were confined and in which over fifty-sex thousand men died. But the general public knew very little about them. I lived in Chicago for fifteen years and remember well talking with friends about the Civil War. The general reaction was "nothing ever happened here in Chicago." So, when I told them that close to two percent of all Confederate deaths were there, they were astounded.

Immediately following the Civil War, much of the ill will between the two sides dealt with the prisoners and their treatment. The only Confederate convicted of war crimes was a prison administrator, and many postwar politicians waved the bloody shirt of having been a POW. Today, we know a fair amount about Andersonville, Belle Isle, Elmira, Camp Douglas, and others; and, recently, several serious scholars have written about the life and death of exchange cartels, the politics concerning African American prisoners, and the logistical failures of both sides to properly feed, cloth, shelter, and provide medical care for the explosion of prisoners in the latter half of the war.

But, until David Keller's research and this book, few have gone beyond the politics and logistics that led to those conditions to explain why those conditions arose and differed from camp to camp, not only North versus South but also within those regions. Keller's research is meticulous. Despite the lack of good data for many of the camps, he developed enough understanding of twenty-six major prisoner of war camps (fifteen in the Confederacy and eleven in the North) to be able to compare them to each other. He then isolated five major factors that could be used to describe the differences among the camps.

In my own mind, I would summarize Keller's research by saying three things. Nobody, North or South, expected so many prisoners. Nobody had any experience to know what to do with them. And the prisoners themselves did not know how to handle their situation.

For the real Civil War buff, this is a wonderful addition to the research that goes far beyond what happened to begin to explain why things happened the way they did. Keller joins a small group of scholars who are proving that there is more to research and write about. Earl Hess has literally and figuratively "dug deeper" to explore how the construction of trenches advanced during the war, and materially affected the fighting, in a series of books. Kent Masterson Brown's *Retreat from Gettysburg: Lee, Logistics & the Pennsylvania Campaign* details the thousands of cattle, sheep, hogs, and tons of foodstuffs that Lee brought back to Virginia with him, giving a different understanding of the grand strategy.

Keller's book belongs in this category. He goes beyond where other scholars have stopped, and he gives us new insights into the deaths of over fifty thousand combatants and the survival of hundreds of thousands of others.

S. Waite Rawls III, Retired President,
American Civil War Museum Foundation

INTRODUCTION

hroughout the Civil War, reports on conditions in prison camps were widely circulated. These reports included death, brutal guards, terrible conditions, and starvation. These negative comments reached their peak in the North in 1864 when photos of Union prisoners released from Belle Isle, a Confederate military prison located in Richmond, Virginia, were received. These images of emaciated solders raised the wrath of the Union government and news media, leading to increased accusations of widespread mistreatment of prisoners by the Confederates.

The introduction to the 1864 United Stated Sanitary Commission report on the Belle Isle prisoners began, "Ever since the outbreak of the war, the country has been full of painful rumors concerning the treatment of prisoners of war by the rebel authorities. Every returned prisoner has brought his tale of suffering, astonishing his neighborhood with an account of cruelty and barbarity on the part of the enemy. Innumerable narratives have also been published and widely circulated." The conclusion of the report confirmed these rumors: "The conclusion is unavoidable, therefore, that 'these privations and sufferings' have been 'designedly inflicted by the military and other authority of the rebel government,' and cannot have been 'due to causes which such authorities could not control.'"[1]

Subsequent reports of death and mistreatment of Union prisoners at Andersonville, Georgia, further fueled condemnation of the Confederacy by the Union government and Northern press.

The Lost Cause became a literary and intellectual movement intended to reconcile the loss by the honorable South to the brutal North. The emergence of the Lost Cause justification by the South is best described by author James Gillispie. "At the end of the Civil War, the South was faced with a rather serious intellectual dilemma. On the one hand there seemed to be evidence that the Richmond authorities, if the testimony given at the Wirz [Commandant of Andersonville Prison] trial was to be believed, had been quite brutal and unchristian toward hapless prisoners of war."[2] This intellectual dilemma resulted in the Lost Cause movement that has colored the history of the Civil War.

The movement intended to maintain the correctness of the Southern lifestyle and to interpret the Civil War as Northern unchristian and brutal treatment of the South and especially the Confederate prisoners. This model grossly overstated starvation and physical abuse and asserted a broad conspiracy to kill Confederate prisoners.

The Lost Cause argument on prisoner treatment was, in part, based on the Jefferson Davis administration report, March 3, 1865, describing prison conditions. The report stated, "in nearly all prison stations of the North . . . our men have suffered from insufficient food and have been subjected to ignominious, cruel, and barbarous practices, of which there is no parallel in anything that has occurred in the South."[3]

The Union kept the issue of treatment of prisoners alive by waving the "bloody shirts" in protest. Many former Union prisoners, to justify pensions, wrote especially graphic details of their prison experiences. The Grand Army of the Republic (GAR) became a significant political factor in postwar America, keeping alive the righteous Union cause.[4] This patter continued boldly through 1879 when James Garfield, future president of the United States, said at an Andersonville reunion, "from Jeff Davis down it was part of their policy to make you idiots and skeletons." That policy, he said, "has never had its parallel for atrocity in the civilized world. We can forgive and forget all other things before we can forgive and forget this."[5]

The characterization of all Civil War prison camps as totally horrible places with starvation and brutality continued in both North and

South narratives through the late twentieth century; recently, however, writers and historians have increased the unbiased knowledge of prisons and prisoners. The following publications informed this book:

Robert Doyle, *The Enemy in Our Hands* (2010), provides an excellent history of enemy prisoners of war (EPW) with special emphasis on conflicts in America, beginning with the French and Indian War (1754–1763). In *Voices from Captivity* (1994) Doyle provides important first-person accounts from prisoners.

James Gillispie, *Andersonvilles of the North: The Myths and Realities of Northern Treatment of Civil War Confederate Prisoners* (2008), discusses in detail many misconceptions about prisoner conditions and treatment during the Civil War, especially the impact of the Lost Cause on the war's reported history.

Roger Peckenpaugh, *Captives in Gray: The Civil War Prisons of the Union* (2009), and *Captives in Blue: The Civil War Prisons of the Confederacy* (2013), offer graphic details on prisons and prison life, most from the perspective of prisoners.

Charles Sanders, *While in the Hands of the Enemy: Military Prisons of the Civil War* (2005), raises several questions about how Civil War prisons were managed during the war, significantly exploring the responsibility of military commanders and political leaders for conditions in the camps.

Lonnie Spear, *Portals to Hell: Military Prisons of the Civil War* (1997), provides illustrative year-by-year details of both Union and Confederate prison camps, showing the evolution of these facilities.

These important historians, as well as a significant number of well-researched books on individual Civil War prison camps, provide a fresh, more balanced look at conditions and causes of conditions in Civil War prison camps. This modern information confirms that the general conditions in all prison camps included poor sanitation, inadequate or poor-quality food and water, lack of proper shelter, primitive medical care, limited clothing, poor supervision, and the poor physical condition of arriving prisoners. A history of any Civil War prison can be written and then, by merely changing the name to any other camp, would be a reasonably accurate description of that second camp. Nearly all prison camps of the period, whether Union or Confederate, had similar shortcomings.

When researching *The Story of Camp Douglas: Chicago's Forgotten Civil War Prison*, I found that all of the negative conditions existed to one degree or another at Camp Douglas. These conditions were a result of five factors: lack of a strategic plan for handling prisoners; inadequate plans for long-term incarceration; poor selection and training of camp command; lack of training of guards; and failure to provide individual soldiers with information on how to behave as a prisoner

Further investigation of other Union and Confederate prisons showed that these factors affected all camps. The research into both Union and Confederate camps was conducted with grants from the Andersonville National Site POW Research Program. Reports were delivered in 2017 and 2018. Complete reports are available for download online at the Andersonville National Historic Site (www.nps.gov/ande/index.htm) and on the website of the Camp Douglas Restoration Foundation (www.campdouglas.org).

Research on Civil War prisons is challenging. While Union records were generally adequate, information on Confederate prisons is sketchy. Based on Union records, for example, it is possible to identify prisons where nearly 75 percent of prison deaths occurred and 80 percent of Confederate prisoners were held (see Appendix III). Confederate records on individual prison deaths and population, except Andersonville, are limited. Moving prisoners from camp to camp to avoid Union military operations and overcrowding of existing prisons resulted often in duplicate prisoner counts, which makes identifying total prisoners held at Confederate camps difficult. With these limitations, Confederate prison camps selected for the study (see Appendix II) are believed to be representative of the Confederate system.

First-person accounts from the young men who fought and survived and the many who died in this great war were extremely important to our understanding conditions and attitudes during the war. The thoughtfulness, thoroughness, and overall quality of their writing provides graphic, firsthand knowledge of the period. Diaries, letters, and journals are an excellent source of first-party observations. Diaries are the most significant; however, these documents represent one person's recollection of the war. Letters are written for the benefit of the receiver. A description of action written to a mother is significantly different from the description of the same event sent to a close pal. Journals offer long detailed descriptions of war events.

Many of these were written well after the war and contain the fragilities of time and selective memory. In addition, some were written to justify military pensions, political ambition, or wartime behavior and are therefore frequently self-serving.

Quotes from prisoners are frequently used here to emphasize material. To assist the reader, a listing of information on all prisoners quoted in the book is provided in Appendix I.

Other information, including newspaper accounts of the day and the government official records, contain excellent information. However, newspapers reflect regional and political bias as well as factual errors. Official records include reports written by individuals with understandable biases. When drawing conclusions from material available, I have used all these sources of information, rather than reaching conclusions from any one source.

The American Civil War created despicable conditions both on the battlefield and in prison camps. Some were caused through neglect, some through malicious intent, and some through the limited knowledge, as well as social and political conditions, of the times. For all examples of brutality, there are examples of compassion and honor. It is important to accept the war for what it was and its players for what they were. There is sufficient blame to go around. Better, we attempt to understand the underlying conditions that caused events between 1861 and 1865.

The purpose of this book is to discuss the five factors that contributed to the conditions of Civil War prisoner of war camps and to discuss how the North and the South reacted to each. Most of these factors were not overtly considered or dealt with by either of the two governments, mainly because of historic precedents of the times. Material reported here is not intended as an indictment of any person or government for failing to understand and react. Rather, the intent is to better understand how prison conditions were affected by ignorance and a misunderstanding of historic events affecting command decisions and prison conditions.

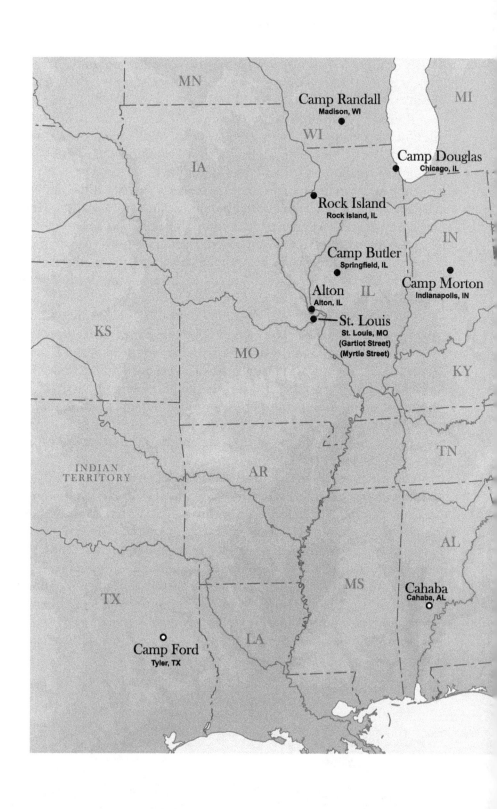

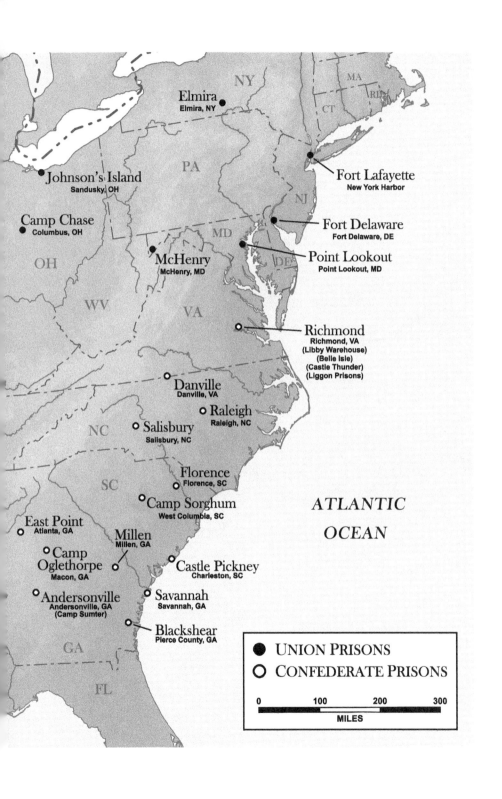

Elmira
Elmira, NY

Fort Lafayette
New York Harbor

Johnson's Island
Sandusky, OH

Fort Delaware
Fort Delaware, DE

Camp Chase
Columbus, OH

Point Lookout
Point Lookout, MD

McHenry
McHenry, MD

Richmond
Richmond, VA
(Libby Warehouse)
(Belle Isle)
(Castle Thunder)
(Liggon Prisons)

Danville
Danville, VA

Raleigh
Raleigh, NC

Salisbury
Salisbury, NC

Florence
Florence, SC

Camp Sorghum
West Columbia, SC

ATLANTIC
OCEAN

East Point
Atlanta, GA

Millen
Millen, GA

Camp
Oglethorpe
Macon, GA

Castle Pickney
Charleston, SC

Andersonville
Andersonville, GA
(Camp Sumter)

Savannah
Savannah, GA

Blackshear
Pierce County, GA

● UNION PRISONS
○ CONFEDERATE PRISONS

0   100   200   300
MILES

CHAPTER 1

IMPACT OF MODERN WARFARE ON THE HISTORY OF PRISONERS OF WAR

In the first third of the nineteenth century, prisoners were not looked upon as people but rather as things. Carl von Clausewitz in his three-volume treatise, *On War*, written in 1832, was silent on the treatment of prisoners. He stated, "Now, in the combat all action is directed to the *destruction* of the enemy, or rather of *his fighting force*, for this lies in the conception of combat." Of prisoners, he advised, "Artillery and prisoners are therefore at all times regarded as the true trophies of victory, as well as its measure, because through these things its extent is declared beyond a doubt."[1]

During the Civil War the poor treatment of prisoners was supported by a variety of institutions. The *Richmond Examiner*, April 30, 1863, recommended, "the Yankee prisoners be put in the cold weather and scant fare will thin them out in accordance with the laws of nature!"[2] The *Chicago Tribune*, February 14, 1862, when contemplating prisoners arriving at Camp Douglas, commented, "If authorities will give Chicago permission to hang the whole bunch as soon as they arrive, let them come."[3]

Not until more than thirty years after the end of the Civil War at The Hague Conference of 1899, ratified by the United States in 1909, was the question of treatment of prisoners of war adequately addressed by the United States as part of the international community.

In fact, prior to the mid-nineteenth century, the phrase "prisoner of war" was inappropriate. Captured combatant was a more fitting description. Field commanders had neither time, resources, nor inclination to handle these captives. Armies during this period emphasized mobility with only modest logistics support. These armies could not manage captives while on the field of battle. The fate of the captured combatants ranged from immediate death to parole. In early warfare, death to all captured soldiers, except senior officers, was applied. In rare instances, captured soldiers were placed into slavery. Influential officers were often ransomed to their governments.

Robert C. Doyle indicates, in *Voices from Captivity*, that in medieval Europe only the wealthy or well-connected were ransomed; the average soldier received a death sentence.[4] As warfare evolved into the eighteenth century, parole became the accepted way to handle captured forces. Under parole, captured combatants agreed, in writing, not to take up arms again until properly exchanged for a member of the opposing army who had likewise been paroled.

The French and Indian War (1754–1763), American Revolutionary War (1775–1783), War of 1812 (1812–1814), and Mexican-American War (1846–1848) set the common attitudes and methods for handling captured combatants in North America.

The French and Indian War was fought with relatively few soldiers supplemented by numbers of Native Americans. The British and Colonial forces never exceeded about seventeen thousand and the French troops were rarely above seven thousand. Captives were frequently subject to massacres with very few treated as prisoners of war. This effect is attributed to the participation of Native Americans and the small unit mobile nature of the conflict. Nothing in the French and Indian War significantly contributed to the ultimate treatment of prisoners of war.

During the American Revolution, Ethan Allen reported in his memoir of his capture in 1775 at Ticonderoga and three-year imprisonment by the British, that the British policy was to kill all prisoners. He estimated that the British killed eleven thousand prisoners during the war.[5]

The American Revolution offered the first glimpse of the conduct of war on the North American continent with management of prisoners of war. In much of that war, parole was the common method of handling those captured. English officers were often paroled in place, living in the colonies at their own expense. The American Continental Army captured an estimated fourteen thousand enemy soldiers and sailors. These numbers severely taxed the Americans' ability to house and feed the captives.[6] This inability to house and feed prisoners supported the institution of parole and exchange. The worst treatment reported during the war was on the British ships that functioned as prisons holding, mostly, American sailors or privateers. Often termed "death ships," prison ships were in Wallabout Bay, New York; Charleston Harbor, South Carolina; and St. Lucia, West Indies.[7] Since most of these prisoners were considered noncombatants, these ship/prisons were exceptions to the routine methods of handling of prisoners.

After the Battle of Kings Mountain (1780), General Washington wrote, "All prisoners taken by Colonel Campbell [at Kings Mountain] have been dismissed, paroled, and enlisted in Militia Service for three months except 130. Thus we have lost by folly, not to say anything worse, of those who had them in charge up to 600 men. I am told Lord Cornwallis has lately made a proposition to General Smallwood for exchange of all prisoners in North and South Carolina. If it is upon terms that are just and equal, I shall avail myself of it for a great number of prisoners is a heavy weight upon our hands."[8]

The Treaty of Amity, ratified in 1785 between the United States and King Frederick the Great of Prussia, was the first time the United States addressed the treatment of prisoners of war. While the treaty was not specific on prisoners, Article 24 generally addressed prisoner treatment. Captors were, for example, to "furnish them with rations as they allow the common soldier in their own service."[9]

The handling of captives during the War of 1812 changed little. The most significant prisoner of war contribution of that war was the creation by British and American representatives of a cartel at a meeting in November 1812 in Halifax, Nova Scotia. This cartel addressed the exchange of prisoners, treatment of noncombatants, treatment of prisoners' well-being, and terms of parole. The 1812 cartel document became the cornerstone for the Dix–Hill Cartel of 1862 between the

Confederate and Union forces (see Appendix IV). The Dix–Hill Cartel, however, was confined to the mechanics of parole and exchange and was silent on the treatment of prisoners. Most noteworthy was the provision that captured prisoners would be paroled within ten days of capture. This provision led to the notion that prisoners would not be held as prisoners of war for extended periods of time.

The Mexican-American War offers little insight into handling prisoners of war. The short, successive battles of this war produced many captives. As many as ten thousand Mexican captives were simply paroled home.[10]

Thus, this was the history of captured combatants at the time of the Civil War. Nothing suggested the need to plan for managing thousands of prisoners of war other than immediate parole and subsequent exchange. It was understandable that military commanders of both armies considered parole as the only acceptable method of handling prisoners.

Prior to the implementation of the Dix–Hill Cartel in July 1862, parole and exchange was negotiated by opposing field commanders. In August 1861, Confederate general Gideon Pillow and Union general Lew Wallace exchanged prisoners in Missouri based on the provisions of the 1812 agreement.[11] In December 1861, US flag officer Lawrence Goldsborough offered Major General Benjamin Huger, Confederate commander at Norfolk, Virginia, a negotiated exchange of Navy and Marine Corps officers avowing secession principles for US Navy officers imprisoned in the South.[12] This exchange was outside the provisions of former conventions and had no relationship to equality of numbers exchanged. A third type of parole was used from time to time. Under this program a captured soldier would be temporarily paroled to allow him to return home and locate an enemy parolee for whom he could be exchanged.[13] These informal exchanges would continue until the Dix–Hill Cartel was issued and in force in mid-1862.

Government leaders and military commanders failed to anticipate that river and rail transportation along with the telegraph development in the early nineteenth century would significantly change not only warfare but the handling of prisoners.

From 1811 until approximately 1830, steamboats replaced small and maneuverable keel boats as the primary commercial river transportation in this country. Beginning in 1827, substantial river improvements, undertaken by the US Army Corps of Engineers, improved long-range free movement of steamboats. This included major improvements in the lower Mississippi, Cumberland, and Tennessee Rivers. By the 1840s the development of steam-powered ships capable of carrying high tonnage of men and supplies became a major mode of transportation throughout the river system of the country.[14] Many of the major rivers were controlled by the Union giving their armies a distinct advantage in the use of steamships and river transportation.

Between 1840 and 1850 railroad track mileage in the US increased from three thousand miles to over nine thousand miles. Much of it was concentrated in the Northeast although some disconnected lines had opened in the Southeast and as far west as Illinois. By the 1850s the locally organized railroads, especially in the North, had been structured into an organized interstate system. In 1851 the telegraph increased the efficiency and coordination of rail transportation.

At the beginning of the Civil War, 30,000 miles of railroads existed, with 21,300 miles concentrated in the Northeast and Midwest while the Confederacy enjoyed only 9,022 miles.[15] The Confederate government was opposed to taking over private enterprises. This hands-off policy produced great confusion and inefficiency in railroads in the South. Speed of southern train travel in 1863 was reduced to ten miles per hour compared to twenty-five miles per hour in 1861.[16]

In 1862, the Union formed the private company, United States Military Railroad (USMR). General Daniel C. McCallum and General Herman Haupt effectively managed this enterprise to ensure the efficiency of the railroad resources of the North in support of the war.[17] The North clearly recognized the importance of railroads to the war effort and used them to their advantage. The South recognized the importance of this resource only later in the war and was not organized to efficiently use this resource.

These changes in transportation provided commanders in the Civil War opportunities to move men and equipment long distances relatively quickly and efficiently. While logistic support for tactical units still depended upon horse and wagon, trains and steamships permitted marshaling supplies faster and closer to the armies, thus reducing the need to carry large quantities of supplies with the moving armies. Improved transportation provided greater mobility and an opportunity to manage prisoners more effectively. Rail and river transportation allowed the military commanders to rapidly move prisoners away from the fighting. This would place tremendous and unseen pressure on prison facilities.

Solon Hyde, 17th Ohio Volunteer Infantry, reported a multiday movement by rail from his capture at Chickamauga in September 1863 to arriving October 11 at the Confederate Libby prison in Richmond. He noted changing trains frequently and traveling in cattle cars.[18] Members of the 11th Illinois noted that transportation from Memphis to Tuscaloosa included rail and small riverboats on the Alabama River.[19]

Union prisoner Lieutenant Joseph Ferguson, recounting his travel from Libby Prison to Lynchburg, Tennessee, in 1864, said, "We were paraded through the streets of the town as if we were wild animals; all the people turned out to see the exhibition. The females smiled on the Home Guards and shook their closed hands at the captive; others contented themselves with dipping snuff and chewing tobacco. These are accomplishments of Southern ladies. The contrast between the rebels and prisoners, in manly bearing, on the display, was in favor of the latter, if they were hatless and shoeless and had their clothing stolen. They looked like men alongside of the scare-crows guarding them." Ferguson continued, "From Lynchburg to Danville we were conveyed in box car, as many as eighty or ninety being placed in a car. The prisoners were actually piled in on each other. These cars had been used in the transportation of animals; before our entrance into them they had not been cleaned or swept, and were in repulsive state of filthiness. There were no window's, holes, or boards knocked off to admit air."[20]

Charles Smedley, in June 1864, reported a thirteen-day trip, mostly by train from Gordonville, Virginia, to Andersonville, Georgia.[21] Smedley would later die after being moved to Florence Prison, Florence, South Carolina, in November 1864.

This ability to move captives quickly and efficiently from the battle, thereby saving commanders time and resources, became the accepted procedure for both the Union and the Confederacy. The creation of prisoner of war camps was a reaction to this improved transportation. Without the foresight of planning for the consolidation and holding of prisoners, each army was forced to react. This change in transportation technology and military commanders taking advantage of it would create and shape significant changes in the movement, housing, and care for prisoners of war for the first time in history.

CHAPTER 2

FIVE FACTORS IMPACTING
PRISONERS OF THE CIVIL WAR

The five factors impacting prisoners of the Civil War considered here are based on studies conducted with the support of Andersonville National Site POW Research Program of the National Park Service. The conclusion of the studies was that five factors impacted all military prisons during the Civil War, regardless of side or geography.

1. LACK OF A STRATEGIC PLAN FOR HANDLING PRISONERS

Prior to the Civil War, few prisoners were held by warring armies. Exchange of prisoners was the usual method of handling captured combatants. Neither the North nor the South planned for prisoners of war in advance. Both sides' failure to anticipate the need to plan for holding prisoners is not surprising. The history of the way prisoners had been handled and the requirement to execute the day-to-day needs of warring armies took precedence. Since both armies were made up mostly of volunteers, mustering in units and providing basic training was the early focus. Training was in weaponry and tactical movement and little else. In the South, the requirement to muster, organize, and equip a new army where none existed before rendered handling prisoners a non-priority.

The understandable lack of an adequate plan for the receipt, transportation, securing, and housing of prisoners would negatively impact all prisoners during the Civil War.

2. INADEQUATE PLANS FOR LONG-TERM INCARCERATION

Under the Dix–Hill Cartel, prisoners were to be paroled within ten days of capture. This requirement proved unworkable but was used as a reason to defer improvements to prison camps by both sides. Only two significant in-place paroles were accomplished: Harper's Ferry by the Confederates in 1862 and Vicksburg by the Union in 1863. As prison populations grew (until two exchanges in mid-1862 and mid-1863) and exploded (after the termination of exchanges in mid-1863) the problems with camps were beyond correction. The South had the added pressure of constantly moving prisoners to inadequate facilities away from overcrowded existing prisons and the advancing Union forces. On-site parole, as anticipated by Dix–Hill, was effectively eliminated by commanders who could move prisoners away from their area of responsibility.

Early in the Civil War, prior to the acceptance of the Dix–Hill Cartel in June 1862, rare parole and exchange was at the discretion of individual commanders. For example, in December 1861, L.M. Goldsmith, commanding, North Atlantic Blockade, negotiated directly with Confederate brigadier general Benjamin Huger offering the exchange of ten Confederate Navy and Marine officers, by name, held by the Union for prisoners held by the Confederacy.[1] Other individually negotiated exchanges were used prior to general exchanges under the Dix–Hill agreement[2]

Two exchanges in 1862 and 1863 were conducted under provisions of Dix–Hill. Except for seriously ill prisoners, all prisoners were efficiently exchanged. Such exchanges were anticipated to continue. In mid-1863 President Lincoln suspended the exchange of Confederate prisoners captured or held in Union prisons. This suspension was a reaction to Jefferson Davis's pronouncement that Union "colored" troops captured would be considered escaped slaves rather than captured soldiers, and white officers commanding these troops would be subject to immediate execution. In addition, Union commanders, especially U.S. Grant complained that paroled Confederate soldiers returned to combat before being properly exchanged. Prisoner exchanges began again only near the end of the war.

After suspension of prisoner exchange until the end of the war, the lack of any planning for long-term incarceration plagued both governments. Deferral of prison camp development resulted in the Union playing catch-up over the next two years. Confederates were forced to continue to expand their prison facilities while especially challenged to keep them out of the reach of Union advances. Even after exhausting hard facilities and depending on open stockades, the Confederacy's capacity for long-term prisoner management was grossly inadequate.

3. POOR SELECTION AND TRAINING OF CAMP COMMAND

Since neither army planned for holding prisoners of war, no commanders were trained for the job. Prison camp commanders were appointed based solely on immediate need, availability, and convenience.

While the Confederacy and Union approached the assignment of commanders differently, neither provided any training for camp commanders. Commander selection, training, and turnover would plague the prison system throughout the war. Although Union and Confederate leadership faced different command challenges, the failure to adequately respond to the importance of command's impact on prisons and prisoners contributed to inadequate care of those incarcerated by either side.

4. LACK OF TRAINING OF GUARDS

None of the guards at Civil War prisons had adequate training on their jobs. Guards were often selected from those readily available, rather than being from troops specifically assigned to the task of guarding prisoners. This resulted in inconsistent, frequently brutal, and undisciplined treatment of prisoners. Guards were often afterthoughts, selected and equipped with minimum consideration for their responsibilities. Often their weapons were obsolete or even condemned. Some guards were armed only with revolvers to manage prisoners. The ratio of guards to prisoners was frequently extremely low, increasing the possibilities of escape or insurrection. There was frequent bribing of guards to facilitate prisoner escapes or special treatment.

Both sides understood the shortcomings of guards assigned to prisons and failed to react to these facts. Training and better guard selection processes could have reduced inhumane treatment of prisoners.

5. FAILURE TO PROVIDE SOLDIERS WITH INFORMATION ON HOW TO BE-
HAVE AS A PRISONER

With no history of holding prisoners, neither army recognized a need
for any training on expected behavior as a prisoner. Armies were
made up of volunteer farmers, clerks, and students who had little understanding of military life, let alone how to behave as a prisoner.
The behavior of some soldiers during the war, both good and bad, is
illustrative of the need to inform soldiers of expectations. Standards
for prisoner behavior were not codified in the US military until the
Code of Conduct was published in 1955.

The following chapters cover each of these five factors in detail,
with special emphasis on how the Union and Confederate armies approached these situations supplemented by the observations of individual soldiers.

CHAPTER 3

CONDITIONS IN CIVIL WAR PRISONS

learly, it can be said that nearly all conditions in the Civil War were deplorable. Put plainly, Civil War prison camps were especially so. During the Civil War more soldiers overall died of disease than combat. It was no different in prison camps. An estimated 30,218 (15.5 percent) Union soldiers died in Confederate prisons. Approximately 25,976 (12 percent) Confederate prisoners died in Union prisons.[1]

Statistics do not support that prisons were significantly worse, or better, than general conditions of the armies. However, Confederate prisoners held in the North were 29 percent less likely to die in the prison camp than with their unit. About 69 percent of Union prisoners held in the South were more likely to die in prison than with their units.[2] Further, the recovery rate from disease for Confederate soldiers held at Union prison Camp Douglas, Chicago, was 94.53 percent compared to 88.6 percent at Richmond's Chimborazo Hospital, the primary care facility for Confederate troops.[3]

Jefferson Davis, president of the Confederacy, in 1890 justified conditions in Confederate prisons:

Without entering into details, the difficulties encountered in the care of the large and, in the latter part of the war, ever-increasing number of prisoners may be briefly enumerated thus:

1. The exceptionally inhuman act of the North, declaring medicines to be contraband, to which there is but one, if indeed there be one, other example in modern war.

2. The insufficient means of transportation and the more inadequate means of repairing railroads and machinery, so that, as the war continued, the insufficiency became more embarrassing.

3. The numerical inferiority of our army made it necessary that all available force should be at the front; therefore the guards for prisons were mainly composed of old men and boys, and but a scanty allowance of these.

4. The medical officers were not more than were required with the troops, and contract physicians disliked the prison service, among other reasons, naturally, because of the impossibility of getting the proper medicines.[4]

President Davis failed to acknowledge that the Confederacy was able to arm, equip, and feed a standing army for over four years. In an 1864 report, the US Sanitary Commission responded to reports of starvation of Union prisoners in Confederate prisons attributed to the lack of food in the South: "One fact was evident on the face of things, that no army could have endured such forced and violent marches, the fatigues and exposures of such desperate campaigning, and have kept up a spirit for such indomitable fighting, unless they had been well-equipped, and their physical condition had been maintained by every means, medical and commissary, known in a well-regulated army. The rebel authorities could not afford to swell their army by conscription on the one hand, and to let the material, thus obtained, escape its military use by famine and disease on the other."[5]

In addition to problems with food during the war, other conditions such as sanitation, clothing, and physical facilities were evident in all prison camps.

Each prison facility faced unique problems and conditions. Yet, similar problems were common in nearly all prisons.

Problems in prison camps were identified early. On September 13, 1861, US Surgeon William J. Sloan reported to Fort Columbus, New York, commander Colonel G. Loomis poor conditions and lack of facilities for over six hundred prisoners. Colonel Loomis forwarded the report to the Headquarters of the Army.[6] There is no response to the report in the Official Record.

LOCATION OF PRISON FACILITIES

Both the Union and Confederates recognized early that prison camps needed to be located near cities and towns away from the fighting. The rail and river systems made this a possibility. Physical facilities ranged from wooden barracks to open fields. Some were repurposed buildings, such as warehouses, existing jails, and military-issued tents. As described by Lonnie Speers in *Portals to Hell: Military Prisons of the Civil War,* the 150 prison facilities could be categorized into seven groups:

1. Existing Jails and Prisons

The South used these facilities extensively early in the war, only to find inadequate numbers available. Jails in Richmond, Virginia, and other southern cities quickly filled to capacity. The limited size and staffing of jails and prisons forced a substantial number of officers to be diverted from the war to jailer duties. Union leaders used civilian jail and prison facilities early in the war to a lesser extent than the Confederacy. Alton Prison in Illinois was the only civilian prison that was operated extensively after the Union converted to mustering in facilities.

2. Coastal Fortifications

The facilities along the Atlantic coast were pressed into service especially by the Union. Fort McHenry, Maryland, Fort Lafayette and others in New York, and Fort Delaware (Maryland/New Jersey) were typical. The Confederates had one of these facilities, Castle Pinckney in Charleston Harbor, Charleston, South Carolina. They were convenient to the extent they were associated with existing military facilities.

3. Old Buildings Converted to Prisons

This type of facility was used extensively by the South. Libby and Liggon Prisons in Richmond and Castle Thunder, Virginia, and tobacco warehouses in Danville, Virginia, are examples. Selection of these facilities raised serious retrofitting problems that would impact prison life. The Union had only a few of these types of facilities. Best known were lesser-used Gartiot Street and Myrtle Street Prisons in St. Louis.

Top, Fort Delaware. Bottom, Castle Thunder, Richmond, Virginia. (*Library of Congress*)

4. Barracks Enclosed by High Fences

These facilities were built on large parcels of land and had been serving as mustering camps for Union forces. High fences, lighting, and guard posts were added to confine prisoners. Camp Douglas; Camp Chase, Ohio; Camp Morton, Indiana; and Camp Butler, Ilinois, were Union examples developed early in the war. Elmira, New York, was added later and Johnson's Island, Ohio, was created, specifically as a prison. These facilities solved a number of the problems of managing prisoners for the Union. Adequate shelter, logistic support, and medical facilities had already been built and were or had been used by Union troops.

The Confederacy used only two of these types of facilities: Raleigh, North Carolina, and Macon, Georgia. Since few of these camps were available in the South, the Confederacy lost the efficiencies of such facilities.

5. Cluster of Tents Enclosed by High Fences
This shoddy method of holding prisoners was used in Belle Isle, Virginia, an island in the James River, and Point Lookout, Maryland, a location adjacent to a major medical facility of the North.

6. Barren Stockades
These cheap and unsatisfactory facilities were used exclusively by the South. The most famous was Andersonville, Georgia, but also included Camp Ford, Texas, and Florence, South Carolina. These poorly planned and undeveloped camps accounted for the greatest number of prison deaths in the Confederate system.

7. Barren Ground
These facilities of open ground surrounded by a guideline of sticks, branches, or ditches were only used in the South. Camp Sorghum, South Carolina, and East Point outside Atlanta were the last hasty attempts by the Confederacy to confine prisoners.[7]

PRISONERS
Civil War soldiers, Union and Confederate, were the young men of the period. In the Union, as many as 50 percent of military aged men served in the war (Illinois, 58 percent; New York, 42 percent; and Massachusetts, 41 percent). A majority of those serving in combat units were between the ages of eighteen and twenty-five. As the war continued, volunteers and draftees were older. The Union Conscription Act of 1863 called for all single men and married men from twenty to thirty-five to be considered Class 1, or the first to be drafted. In April 1862, the Confederates enacted the first conscription in the US, and men from eighteen to thirty-five were subject to three years of military service. Both sides provided for "buying" a substitute for service.

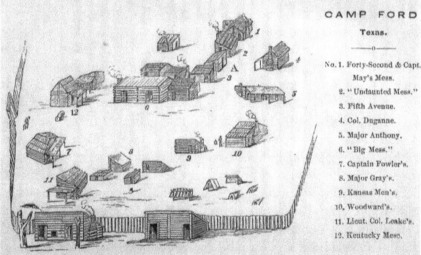

CAMP FORD
Texas.
—0—

No. 1. Forty-Second & Capt.
May's Mess.
2. "Undaunted Mess."
3. Fifth Avenue.
4. Col. Duganne.
5. Major Anthony.
6. "Big Mess."
7. Captain Fowler's.
8. Major Gray's.
9. Kansas Men's.
10. Woodward's.
11. Lieut. Col. Leake's.
12. Kentucky Mess.

Top, Elmira, New York. (*Library of Congress*) Bottom, plan of Camp Ford, Texas. (*National Archives*)

By 1860, the rural population in the North had shrunk to nearly 40 percent while in the South 80 percent of the population was located in rural areas. In the North, 47.5 percent of farmers and laborers participated in the war. This group comprised 42.9 percent of the men in the1860 census. Skilled and unskilled laborers made up 41 percent of participants and 41.6 of the male population in 1860. In the South, farmers and farm laborers constituted 61.5 percent of the fighting men compared to 57.5 percent in the 1860 census. Skilled and unskilled laborers were 22.6 percent of participants and 28.4 percent of the 1860 male population.[8]

In 1860, nearly 90 percent of free Northerners were literate and 80 percent in the South, thus both armies were provided with soldiers of relatively high reading and writing skills. Recruiting of units by both sides tended to be local in scope. A regiment, consisting of approximately a thousand men, was frequently recruited in towns or from neighborhoods in cities. The nucleus for the Confederate army was made of state militia units that had been initially formed before the war. In the Union army, ethnic and special interest groups also tended to be recruited together. Units of Irish and German immigrants were common in the North and from rural settlements in the South. This local recruiting resulted in brothers, cousins, and fathers often recruited into the same units. As a result, if units were captured, family members were often incarcerated together.

The officer corps of the Union consisted, first, of graduates from the US Military Academy at West Point, New York. This group constituted the senior officers at the rank of colonel or general. West Point graduates were supplemented by civilians in the recruiting of regiments. Typically, with the rank of colonel, these officers were appointed by state governors. Many of these civilian officers later rose to the rank of general and performed well; others were released from service after unsatisfactory performance. The last groups of senior officers were political appointees. These generals frequently lacked any military skills and were often ineffective as military commanders. Major General Benjamin Butler, Major General Nathan Banks, and Major General John McClernand are examples from this group of officers. General McClernand performed acceptably as a military commander; however, his constant involvement in political intrigue made his effectiveness unsatisfactory, leading to his removal from service.

Company officers (lieutenants and captains) were routinely elected by members of their units. These men, frequently enlisted as privates, were most often better educated than the average soldier and were sometimes involved in recruiting efforts. Some officers were promoted from the ranks after regiments were formed and combat losses were incurred.

Confederate officer selection was similar to that of the Union. General officers were appointed by the central government. Nearly 30 percent of officers who reached the rank of general in the Confederate army were graduates of West Point.[9] Southern military schools such as Virginia Military Institute (VMI) and The Citadel provided a number of additional general officers. Like the North, the Confederacy had a number of political generals, such as Major General Gideon Pillow and Lieutenant General Leonidas Polk. Polk, a graduate of West Point in 1827 who resigned shortly after graduation, and Pillow proved to be important political appointments to Jefferson Davis but poor military leaders.

Other Confederate field officers, major through colonel, were usually part of the state militia units mustered into Confederate service. As with the Union, company officers were customarily elected by men in the units.

The average age of general officers in the Civil War was thirty-nine.[10] The age of other officers was significantly less, and the average soldier was in his mid-twenties.

The reason for enlisted men volunteering for the armies ranged from social pressure to a lust for adventure. Most of the soldiers did not have a political motive for joining. Most of the population, North and South, had a stronger allegiance to their individual states than to the nation. The closest politics came to encouraging enlistment was in the South where the strongest identification with individual states was present. Upon states seceding, many recruits joined for the protection of their state from possible invasion from the North. Few of the Confederate common soldiers held slaves or strongly supported slavery.

Often, when the recruits entered the army, it was the first time they left their homes. Little was known about the world outside their small sphere of experience. Confederate soldiers, who were essentially rural inhabitants, were subjected, for the first time, to many communicable diseases, such as measles and mumps, illnesses associated with larger dense populations in cities and towns. This would prove a significant medical risk for many in the prison setting.

When captured, officers and enlisted men were separated as soon as possible. Most Confederate officers were sent to prisons specially selected for officers. Johnson's Island, near Sandusky, Ohio, was the

largest, with some officer prisoners held at the Ohio State Penitentiary, and Fort Delaware, Maryland. Where enlisted men and officers
were held at the same prison, such as Fort Delaware and Camp Douglas, officers were housed in different locations from the enlisted.
Union officers were held most often in Libby Prison, Richmond; Castle Pinckney, Charleston; Blackshear Prison, Blackshear, Georgia, and
a few other locations. In these locations, when housed in facilities
that included the enlisted, officers were segregated from the enlisted
men. As a general rule, conditions in officer facilities were better than
those of the enlisted men.

Union lieutenant Alonzo Cooper in the introduction to his memoirs noted, "I suffered but little in comparison with what was endured
by the rank and file, our numbers being less, our quarters were more
endurable and our facilities for cleanliness much greater."[11] This is
partially due to a mutual respect for rank and the cooperative attitude
of the officer prisoners. With Johnson's Island representing a specially planned facility for officers, Confederate officer prisoners had
better facilities than their Union counterparts.

When viewing enlisted Confederate prisoners in Union prisons,
there are some clear distinctions. One group of prisoners' homes or
families were in border states and states that were under Union control during most of the war. While contested, Tennessee and Kentucky were mostly in Union hands. Arkansas and Missouri had
guerilla warfare during much of the war, but most of the area was
controlled by the Union. This offered prisoners with families living
in these areas the availability of US mail and visits. Not only did this
offer them the comfort of contact with home but packages with food,
clothing, and money provided them with special opportunities for
goods and supplies not available to others. These groups of "haves"
rarely were hungry and offered a perspective of not living with the
deprivation of others.

A subgroup of these prisoners were members of the units without
outside contact. Some prisoners may not have had access to the outside because of a lack of family or a family outside the protection of
the Union, but they had comrades from their unit that were more
likely to share their bounty than with a stranger.

The "Galvanized Yankees," or those who signed the Oath of Allegiance, were yet another subgroup of the "haves." Often with special

Top, non-commissioned officers, 19th Iowa Infantry, exchanged prisoners from Camp Ford, Texas. Bottom, Confederate prisoners captured at cavalry fight at Aldie, Virginia, June 1864. (*Library of Congress*)

privileges including improved living conditions, duties, and food, this group was isolated from the general prison population. Few of these men maintained a diary or journal. Some other prisoners obtained money from the sale of their artwork and can be considered a subgroup of this group. Prisoners with little contact outside the camp or little opportunity to receive packages could improve their lot with jobs in the prison, such as cooks, clerks, and orderlies, which offered special privileges. The "Free Masons" were frequently mentioned by prisoners who received special treatment from "Free Mason" guards. They are considered in the group of "haves." Clearly advantages of this group varied within the subgroups and as a result of actions and policies at individual prisons.

The final group of prisoners was those with none of the advantages of other prisoners. Alone, with no contact with their home and family, these soldiers were subject to having available to them what was left. Unless the "haves" shared with these "have nots," life was exceptionally bleak. The probability of illness because of lack of proper food and exposure to wretched conditions was highest among this group.

Prisoners from each of these groups had a different perspective of prison life and presented that perspective differently.

Union enlisted prisoners in Confederate prisons had fewer "haves" as a result of less frequent availability of mail, family support, and frequent movement to other camps. Most of the support came from those in their own units or contacts made in prison. These contacts were less intense than those in Confederate units. The Oath of Allegiance to the Confederacy was infrequently used by Union prisoners, and there was no evidence of special treatment in the prisons. Jobs within the prisons were limited and offered few opportunities for Union prisoners. Artwork sold by prisoners was fairly common and Union soldiers took great care in protecting money on hand or obtained from guards and camp personnel for their art. It can generally be said that Union prisoners were more often considered "have nots."

These then were the prisoners who would be subjected to the horrors of incarceration for four long years.

FACILITIES, SHELTER, AND CLOTHING

Each prison camp had unique problems, ranging from organization to maintenance and upkeep. Frequently, the facilities were initially adequate only to be pressed to significant overcrowding and disrepair. Deferred maintenance in the North and the press of military operations on the Confederacy often interfered with constructing or maintaining adequate facilities. Both the Union and Confederacy were faced with these realities that were made worse as the prison populations grew.

Curtis Burke, upon arriving at Camp Douglas in mid-1863 reported,

> All of the barracks were long one story buildings. Four of them forming a square with a cook house on the outside of the square to each barrack and the length of the barrack. The barracks were divided into little rooms with from two to ten bunks in each, and doors and windows to match, also one long room with a row of bunks on each side of the room, mostly three bunks deep or high, and making room for about eighty men. There was a general stampede of our boys to secure the little rooms. My mess of four decided to go in a little room with three of company C. to fill it up making seven in all in the room. It was [illegible] feet wide by twenty-five feet long. A door and window front and a window back.
>
> We nailed up a cracker box and three shelves to put our rations and other tricks on. There was a table ready made in the room when we came. I made a stout bench about seven feet long from planks I found laying around. We opened both windows and door to let the fresh air pass through. There was a plank pavement in front of our door about three feet wide. We received rations of crackers, bread, bacon, pickelled pork, coffee, sugar, potatoes, hominy, salt, soap, and candles. Of course, a man only got a handful of each when it was divided, but we received better rations here than we did at Camp Morton, Ind.[12]

Southern prisons located in abandoned factories and warehouses lacked adequate toilet facilities and fresh water. Some lacked sufficient light and ventilation. Retrofitting these facilities was difficult and expensive; many of the basic facility improvements were either not provided or were inadequate. Plus, as the war continued, abandoned factories and warehouses were no longer available. The South then depended upon barren stockades as prisons. S. M. Dufur, a Union prisoner at Florence, South Carolina, in 1864 reported, "After we had remained there six or eight weeks, the rebels erected three sheds, forty or fifty feet in length. They were erected in one corner of the stockade and used for a hospital. There were no walls to these sheds excepting the posts, and when it rained and the wind blew, the inmates were nearly as bad off as if they were outside."[13]

On the Union side, inadequate latrines often plagued prisoners in the camps. In early 1862, at Camp Douglas, sinks, or latrines, were twenty feet long, six feet wide, and four feet deep, running in the middle of White Oak Square where prisoners were housed. Dr. A. M. Clark, medical inspector of prisons, in October 1863 found these sinks with "No management at all, in filthy conditions."[14] The methods of food preparation, often changed within the camps, frequently resulted in poor-quality food provided to the prisoners. These causes ranged from mess facilities that often deployed questionable cooking equipment with poor sanitation to prisons where individual prisoners received food and were left to prepare it. This later resulted in uneven delivery of rations.

At Camp Douglas, in 1863, Colonel William Hoffman, commissary of Union Prisons, ordered the use of "Farmer's Boilers," which were crude boilers that replaced stoves in the cooking areas. Colonel Hoffman stated, "The Farmer boilers are in use in several camps under my charge and are found to be the most convenient mode of cooking, and if they have failed at Camp Douglas it is because those who used them did not want to succeed."[15] This is a clear example of blaming the prisoners for their plight. These boilers proved unsuccessful, as described by Camp Douglas quartermaster Captain Shurley, "Quite a number of the Farmers boilers used for cooking are unfit for use." Camp commander Colonel Charles De Land reported to Colonel Hoffman, "We have tried the Farmer boilers and they are a failure."[16] Prisoners were not pleased with the quality of food cooked in the boilers. Prisoner John Copley described the results as, "a little pittance of meat, which had been boiled to shreds until it contained no more substance than an old dish-rag would."[17]

In September 1861, Leroy Warren reported being held in Richmond's Atkinson's Tobacco House as a prisoner. He described the warehouse as, "a five story brick building, about 80 feet long by forty wide, with a projection on the backside. I hardly know whether to call it a factory or warehouse. . . . In the lower story, which we occupy, are forty or more screw presses which were used to reduce the raw tobacco leaf to a plug form. . . . The fifth story, which is not used as a prison, contains tobacco in various forms as our boys found out."[18] The hasty use of this facility provided Union soldiers with tobacco, a valuable medium of exchange.

In July 1865, describing Libby Prison in Virginia, Junius Browne, correspondent for the *New York Tribune* and prisoner, wrote, "we had

Gen. William Hoffman, Commissary General of Prisoners (right) and staff on the steps of his office in Washington, DC. (*Library of Congress*)

no tables, except the rough boards from which we ate, and they were always in use; no chairs, or stools, or boxes even, to sit upon; no space, however small, which was free from invasion and disturbance."[19] Brown later described the quarters at Salisbury, North Carolina. "The quarters in which we were confined were very undesirable, being about ninety by forty feet, with barred windows, dirty floor, partially occupied by rude bunks, and two broken stoves that gave out no heat, but a perpetual smoke of green pine-wood that made the atmosphere blue, and caused us to weep as though we had lost the dearest mistress of our soul."[20]

Belle Isle, located in the James River in Virginia, within sight of Libby Prison, consisted of four to five acres surrounded by a putrid ditch. A November 1863 report indicated that Belle Isle contained 6,300 prisoners whose condition was "wretched beyond all description." An insufficient number of tents to protect the men from the cold and rain, no blankets nor bedding given them by their captors.[21]

Lieutenant A. C. Roach, incarcerated at Libby Prison, observed in the winter of 1863–1864,

The prisoners on Belle Isle had neither barracks, tents, or shelter of any kind furnished them, until about mid-winter, when a few old worthless tents, too ragged and torn to keep out either wind, rain or snow, perhaps enough to accommodate one-fifth of the men, was given them. In the meantime, however, they had made excavations in the sand, with pieces of bone, sticks of wood, and in many instances with their fingers alone, as no tools or material to construct a shelter were allowed them, nor any means of living as civilized men, nor way of helping themselves as savages.[22]

Roach went on to comment, "No sooner were our men made prisoners, than they were robbed of their blankets, overcoats and money. Many of them were robbed of their hats, shoes, coats and pantaloons, and arrived at Richmond with but their shirts and drawers to cover their nakedness."[23]

Upon arriving at Camp Douglas in January 1863, Private Robert Bagby, 1st Northwest Missouri Cavalry, wrote, "The weather was cool and cloudy. We were still riding when the daylight came. I had slept but little during the night last. I smelt a terrible smell. We passed over some very fine country just before we entered in Chicago about 11:00. Before we got out of the cars many had crammed around the cars and one fellow remarked that the prisoners all should be hung. He had no more than said it until some Irishman had knocked him down. There liked to be a general riot. Finally we were marched out to Camp Douglas which is on or near Lake Michigan shore. There were at least 170 or 180 prisoners of us."[24]

Physical problems at most camps continued to be common. At Camp Douglas, in October 1863, the one hydrant supplying water was not working; rations for the prisoners were slow in arriving, and the barracks needed repairs. At that time camp commander colonel De Land reported to Colonel Hoffman that he was spending a considerable time and effort, mostly with prisoner help, improving the barracks and installing the water and sewage system that General Montgomery Meigs, quartermaster general, who had overall responsibility for Union prisons, had provided belated approval for in June.[25]

In 1863, when Secretary of War Edwin M. Stanton refused to provide funds for barracks at the Point Lookout, Maryland, prison, Point Lookout became the only Union prison to use tents for shelter year

Five unidentified Confederate prisoners at Camp Douglas, Chicago. (*Library of Congress*)

round.[26] These Sibley tents were designed for twelve Union soldiers but housed as many as eighteen Confederates. Prisoner James T. Wells recalled, "Our tents were miserable affairs, being full of holes and very rotten. They were of the Sibley pattern and into each one of these sixteen men were so crowded. In order to lay down at night the men were compelled to lay so close together as to exclude sleep."[27]

J. Osborn Coburn, prisoner on Belle Isle in November 1863, reported, "All but about 500 are now in tents, but without blankets or wood the cold is intense."[28] Yet, Confederate major Isaac Carrington issued in an inspection report November 18, 1863, stating that "Belle Isle prisoners are comfortable clothed, well fed, and their sanitary needs provided for."[29]

W. F. Lyons described the following at Andersonville: "We were without clothing, without shelter, exposed to the burning sun by day and to the cold at night, for in that part of the South the nights are very cool, while the heat during the day is intense. My wardrobe consisted of a woolen shirt, a pair of cotton flannel drawers, a pair of army pantaloons, a pair of boots and the old hat which I was compelled to take in exchange for my good one when I was captured. I had no blanket, no shelter of any kind by night or day, save when I begged the privilege of sitting in my friend's mud shanty during the hottest part of the day."[30]

Andersonville lacked any order. Prisoner-built "shebangs" consisted of twigs and mud, personal clothing, and equipment. Nothing was provided by the camp. The camp was so disorganized that roll calls were very difficult. Prisoner Charles Smedley wrote of roll call at Andersonville in June 1864, "Had roll-call this forenoon, the first time for three weeks it was difficult to get the men together, and was eleven o'clock before they got through."[31]

Major John O. Murray, Confederate prisoner at Fort Delaware in August 1864 reported, "On the grounds of the island were built large wooden barracks separated into compartments, one of which was occupied by the Confederate officers"[32] Later at Morris Island (Charleston Harbor) Prison he reported being assigned to "tents, putting four men in each small A-tent which would not comfortably hold more than two men."[33]

Lieutenant Alonzo Cooper, Union prisoner, described Danville Prison in late 1864. "Danville in 1864-5 was a town of considerable importance to the Confederacy, being the base of supplies for the Confederate army at Richmond and Petersburg. There were three or four military prisons there, in which were confined about two thousand enlisted men, captured from the Union forces, and four hundred officers. They were all confined in tobacco warehouses in different parts of the city, the officers being separate from the enlisted men."[34]

Arriving at Salisbury Prison in 1864, Colonel Homer Sprague, 18th Connecticut Volunteers, described his quarters: "Salisbury prison, then commonly called 'Salisbury penitentiary,' was in the general form of a right-angled triangle with base of thirty or forty rods, perpendicular eighty or ninety. In a row parallel to the base and four or five rods from it were four empty log houses with a space of about four rods between each two. These, a story and a half high, had formerly been negro quarters. On each side of the great triangle was a stout tight board fence twelve or fifteen feet high. Some two or three feet from the top of this, but out of our sight because on the other side, there was evidently a board walk, on which sentinels, four or five rods apart, perpetually paced their beats, each being able to see the whole inside of the enclosure. At each angle of the base was a shotted field-piece pointing through the narrow opening."[35]

A group of huts at Andersonville, Georgia, known as "Mud Island." To the right is the "dead-line" where prisoners would be shot if they entered it. (*Library of Congress*)

In July 1863, Lieutenant Colonel Charles Farnsworth, 1st Connecticut Cavalry, reported, "Upon reaching the Libby, we were rigidly searched, and all moneys and attractive jack-knives, nice overcoats and meerschaum pipes were kindly appropriated by the prison authorities; rubber blankets, canteens, spurs and haversacks were taken from us. Lieut. Moran, for complaining of this treatment, was knocked down by Richard Turner, inspector of the prison clothing. There was never an issue of clothing or blankets made by the Confederate authorities during the time I was there confined [March 1864]."[36]

W. F. Lyon, upon arrival at Camp Oglethorpe in Macon, in 1864, described it, saying, "We were placed in Camp Oglethorpe, a fair ground, and were furnished with shelter tents, no stockade having then been built there, and were furnished with rations of salt pork and corn bread."[37]

Confederate prisoner Creed T. Davis, in April 1865, reported at the temporary prison camp at City Point, Virginia: "a tent was issued to every six men, a better tent than we have ever seen in the Confederate army."[38]

In the winter of 1863, prisoners at Camp Morton, Indiana, were reported as having few blankets and little straw for bedding. They were required to huddle together "spooning" for warmth.[39]

In November 1863, Dr. William F. Swalm of the Sanitary Commission reported, "They [prisoners at Point Lookout, Maryland] are poorly supplied with blankets and they must have suffered severely from the cold, for it is a very bleak place. Generally they have one blanket to three men, but a great many are entirely without."[40]

Soldiers from Roman legions to today's modern soldier have shed bulky and unneeded equipment. During the Civil War, rubber blankets, overcoats, and extra clothing were often abandoned or left in bivouac areas by both the Union and Confederate soldiers. Prisoners frequently were captured with minimum clothing and comfort equipment such as blankets and shelter halves. This condition was especially harmful to Confederate prisoners who were transported from moderate temperatures to cold weather locations in the North.

On February 22, 1862, the *Chicago Tribune* reported on prisoners arriving from the surrender of Fort Donelson, a Confederate stronghold on the Cumberland River in Tennessee. "A more woebegone appearing set of men it would be difficult for a reader to imagine. The uniforms were considered inadequate, and intended for a warmer climate with some have coats of butternut. Many of them have no overcoats at all and supply their place with horse blankets, hearth rugs, coverlids, pieces of carpet, coffee sacks, etc. etc." [41]

"During January [1863]," testified Private George Dingman of the 27th Michigan Infantry, prisoner at Belle Isle, "men would run all night to keep warm, and in the morning I would see men lying dead."[42]

Colonel Michael Corcoran, 69th New York Infantry, captured at Bull Run in 1861, reported from Liggon Prison in Richmond, "We are all in great need of clothing here and in many cases without a single cent to procure any of the different things absolutely necessary."[43]

Much of the clothing provided to Confederate prisoners had been condemned and rejected as unfit for issue to Union Soldiers.[44] Prisoner Curtis Burke at Camp Douglas described the clothing provided to prisoners who were leaving the smallpox hospital and returning to their barracks: "We then had to throw away our old, but warm clothes and put on our new suits of blue, consisting of thin shoes without socks, unlined pants without drawers, a good gray shirt and a thin frock coat with the tail trimmed with scissors or a knife into a clawhammer or spade tail, looking very odd. Every other button was also cut off. All kept their old hats. Our toilet at last completed by tieing our cravats (if we had one) A La Brummel."[45]

On August 12, 1863, Colonel Hoffman ordered, "You will issue no clothing of any kind except in case of utmost necessity. So long as a prisoner has clothing upon him, however much torn, you must issue nothing to him, nor must you allow him to receive clothing from any but members of the immediate family, and only when they are in absolute want."[46]

Facilities for maintaining existing clothing were frequently inadequate. Union lieutenant Alonzo Cooper, at Macon, reported, "Our facilities for washing and boiling our clothing was very limited, and nothing but boiling them would have any effect in exterminating these troublesome pests [lice]; soap was a scarce commodity, and kettles for heating water were difficult to obtain, so the only way to rid ourselves of vermin, was to strip off our woolen shirt."[47]

Frequently, local residence and sanitary commissions attempted to supplement the government issue of clothing and bedding. While worthy efforts, they provided little to solve the problem of inadequate clothing. In November 1864, General U. S. Grant and Judge Robert Ould, Confederate Agent of Exchange, reached an agreement to allow Confederate General Nelson Beall, named CS Army Agent to Supply Prisoners of War, to sell Southern cotton that was allowed through the Union blockade. The thousand bales of cotton would be sold in New York, and Beall was then authorized to purchase goods for the benefit of Confederate prisoners held in Northern prisons. None of the proceeds from the sale were to benefit anyone in the Confederacy except the prisoners. Upon the sale of the cotton, after taxes and expenses, General Beall had $332,789.66 to spend on over 13,000 pairs of pants, 13,200 blankets, 11,175 pairs of shoes, and other items of clothing that were distributed to Confederate captives in Union prisons.[48]

In spite of these attempts, prisoners were often inadequately dressed.

FOOD

Adequacy or inadequacy of rations in Civil War prisons is open to interpretation. The stated policy of both sides was to provide food to prisoners equal to that available to their own troops. Some items, such as candles, were included in Union "rations" and then withheld because they were used in tunneling escape attempts. This resulted in reports of reduced rations.

The recommended diet, both in North and South, was about 2,325 calories, including 75.5 grams of protein and 77.5 grams of fat for garrison troops per day. Authorized prisoner rations provided a range from 1,400 to 3,000 calories, 30 to 245 grams of fat, and 40 to 165 grams of protein, depending upon the alternatives provided.[49] The authorized diet failed to provide adequate vitamins and minerals needed except for niacin. These deficiencies, principally the lack of fruits and vegetables, contributed to the incidence of disease, especially scurvy, in the camps.

The table opposite is a summary of authorized prison rations in Union prisons.

Based on prisoner comments on the food, both the quantity and quality of the "official" rations were questionable.

William D. Huff, a prisoner at Camp Douglas in June 1864, wrote "They [prison guards] have taken our cooking vessels from us and instituted kitchens and shortened our rations giving us nothing but pork and bread and not quite enough of that. I do not mean fresh pork oh, no, but salt pickled pork full of fat and not water enough to wash it down."[51]

J. Osborn Coburn, a Union prisoner at Belle Isle, reported in November 1863 that prisoners were "starving."[52] On November 12 he wrote that rations consisted of "8 ounces of boiled rice for breakfast: at noon we got rations of bread. At night we got no sweet potatoes as did many of the squads but double of corn and bread."[53] In January 1864, Coburn's fellow prisoner John Ransom reported, "Beans were very wormy and musty. Hard work finding a bean without from one to three bugs in it. They were put in a large caldron kettle of river water and boiled for a couple of hours. No seasoning, not even salt to put into them."[54]

Rations for Confederate prisoners at Fort Delaware were reported to be a three-inch-long and one-inch-thick piece of cornbread, yellow

Rations per Prisoner*	April 20, 1864	June 1, 1864	Jan. 13, 1865	1861 Confederate Authorized Daily Ration
Pork or Bacon, or	10 oz.	10 oz.	10 oz.	12 oz.
or Fresh or salt beef	14 oz.	14 oz.	14 oz.	20 oz.
Flour or bread (soft)	18 oz.	18 oz.	16 oz.	18 oz.
or Hard bread,	14 oz.	14 oz.	10 oz.	12 oz.
or Corn meal	18 oz	18 oz.	16 oz.	20 oz.
Rations per 100 prisoners				
Beans or peas or	6 qt.	12.5 lbs.	12.5 lbs.	8 qt.
or Rice or Hominy	8 lbs.	8 lbs.	8 lbs.	10 lbs.
Coffee, green	7 lbs.	**	**	6 lbs.
or Coffee roasted and Ground	5 lbs.	**	**	**
or Tea	18 lbs.			
Sugar	14 lbs.	**	**	12 lbs.
Vinegar		3	2 qt.	4 qt.
Candles				
Soap				
Salt				
Molasses				
Potatoes				

*Prisoners in public works received slightly higher quantities of rations.

**Sugar, coffee, or tea issued to sick and wounded only, every other day, on recommendation of surgeon in charge, at a rate of 12 pounds of sugar, 5 pounds of ground or 7 pounds of green coffee, or 1 pound of tea to every 100 rations.[50]

in color, a small piece of bacon or beef, and a cup of logwood and beans called coffee for breakfast. Dinner was slightly more food, including pickled beef soup. The meat was often spoiled and covered with flies.[55]

In September 1864, Curtis R. Burke, Camp Douglas prisoner, reported a shortage of rations. "We had hash for dinner, but hardly enough to do any good. We are getting boiled beef for dinner and breakfast eight days out of ten, and as we draw beef at dinner for breakfast also, we eat it all up for dinner without trouble and have bread and water for breakfast."[56]

In 1864 prisoner Major George Putnam described rations at Libby Prison: "Large or small, the chunk [of meat] was not even nourishing throughout. The cake as baked contained other things besides cornmeal. Pieces of the corn-cob were ground up indiscriminately and we also found in the cake cockroaches and other insects and occasionally pieces of mice that had lost their way in the meal-bins."[57]

Union prisoner lieutenant A. C. Roach described the enlisted food at Libby Prison as, "The soup was brought in to the prisoners in wooden buckets, and I have frequently noticed it when the top was covered with white maggots that the process of cooking had forced from the meat and beans."[58]

Prisoner Solon Hyde reported the following food at Confederate Danville Prison: "The rations issued to us after the first few days were of the poorest kind and revoltingly cooked. It was a very common thing to find rat-dung cooked in the rice; our pea soup, made from a kind of black pea cultivated abundantly through the South, and fully ripe when gathered, was always covered with pea bugs, which floated on top; cabbage soup was sometimes substituted for pea soup, and this was worse, if possible, than the other."[59]

Major John O. Murray, Confederate officer held prisoner at Fort Delaware in September 1864 stated, "Our rations, under this order [Dated September 7, 1864, By order of Col. William Gurney, 127th N. Y. Vols. commanding post], was a menu for wooden gods. It consisted of four hardtack army crackers, often rotten and green with mold, and one ounce of fat meat, issued to us at morning roll call; for dinner, we received one-half pint of bean or rice soup, made as the caprice of the cook suggested."[60]

Even captured generals complained about rations. Union brigadier general Neal Dow wrote in his diary January 22, 1864, at

Libby Prison, "The only ration served out is 1/2 a small loaf of miserably made corn bread-heavy as lead-of unsifted meal and 1/2 gill of rice. The latter not every day. No meat of any kind. A small piece of soap (miserable) once a month and a half, and 2 or 3 very wretched tallow candles."[61]

Lieutenant Alonzo Cooper showed frustration regarding rations in 1864 at Danville when he wrote,

> Danville was at this time, the depot of supplies for Lee's army at Richmond, and contained a large amount of Artillery and ammunition; besides having storehouses, well stocked with captured hard tack, so that there would be no lack of supplies for our army. We were therefore, actually dying of starvation in the midst of plenty. In going daily from the prison to the river for water, we passed a building 20 x 40 feet, two stories high, that was packed from bottom to top with captured U.S. hard tack, and others filled with bacon, and other provisions; and tried to get Colonel Smith, commanding the prisons, to give us rations of hard tack once or twice a week, but were told that this was held for the use of their troops in the field.[62]

In April 1865, Confederate soldier Creed T. Davis reported prison rations at City Point: "Our rations are codfish and hard navy crackers."[63]

At Andersonville, when raw rations were issued, prisoners had to have fuel, which became scarce, for cooking. An Ohio orderly sergeant complained the first day he drew rations consisting of only a small piece of cornbread and two bits of meat.[64] In the spring of 1862, rations at Cahaba (Dallas County, Alabama) were described by Union prisoners as very poor pickled beef and a cup full of mush.[65]

Prisoner W. H. Lightcap described rations at Andersonville: "The Rebs called the mess hog peas, but they were small black beans, cooked as they were pulled, vines, pods and all together. Near the northwest corner of the stockade there was a cook house where they were boiled in very large cast iron kettles."[66]

The situation in Andersonville was so critical that Confederate general Winder, on July 25, 1864, wrote Adjutant General Samuel Cooper, "There are 29,400 prisoners, 2,650 troops, 500 negroes and other laborers and not a ration at the post."[67]

In most writings by Civil War soldiers, food was second only to weather in mentions in diaries. Part of the problem with food can be attributed to inadequate methods of storing fresh food. This problem also plagued the average field soldier. Spoilage and insect infestation were common throughout the war. Problems with purveyors shorting rations or providing substandard cuts of meat were mentioned frequently. This fraud was rarely identified by ineffective quartermaster supervision. Undoubtedly, prison food quality was frequently below even low field expectations.

A case in point about civilian vendors occurred at Camp Douglas. In 1864, commanding officer General William W. Orme noted that one subcontractor's beef had been short "for some time back." However, he noted the "fraud" and "cheating of weight" lacked sufficient evidence to warrant prosecution. He required Mr. Curtis, the subcontractor in question, to make restitution for the shortages. Upon investigation, he found that all other contractors were not involved in the matter, one of whom was Ninian Edwards, who was married to Elizabeth Todd Edwards (the older sister of Mary Todd Lincoln) and deeply involved in Illinois politics. Edwards was an active supporter of President Lincoln, who, in turn, had been instrumental in Edwards' appointment as commissary of subsistence for Illinois with the rank of captain.[68]

Frequently, commanders identified problems with food acquisition and distribution only to find that administrative red tape delayed corrective action. In early July 1862, Captain Benjamin Walker, at Camp Chase, Ohio, was charged as significantly deficient in his duties as commissary officer. His poor administration, frequent absence, and acceptance of substandard rations were reported to Colonel Hoffman's office. Investigations into Captain Walker's behavior continued until September 22 when he was dismissed from the service. In the meantime, substandard rations continued to be delivered to prisoners at Camp Chase. Even after dismissal, the case of Captain Walker took on political overtones with Indiana congressman Schuyler Colfax inquiring of President Lincoln why Captain Walker was dismissed.[69]

Even living under these life-threatening problems with food, humor came through. Lieutenant Joseph Ferguson, 1st New Jersey, while a prisoner in Savannah reported, "A ludicrous scene one day occured in camp. A very large hog happened to get t'through the guardline, and when he was inside of the dead-line (in fact there was no dead-line; a small stake was driven in the ground here and there around camp, and none knew where the terrible line was) a rush was made for his porkship by the meat-hungry officers. In a shorter time than it would take to tell how, he was divided into hundreds of pieces."[70]

It is difficult to determine whose food, North or South, was worse; similar complaints were received from field soldiers in both armies. Certainly, neither consistently met the authorized quantity of rations, and quality was below acceptable standards.

PRIMITIVE MEDICAL CARE

While medical facilities were usually available to prisoners, these facilities were often inadequate. Medical facilities at most Union camps were a part of prison facilities or adjacent to them. Confederate medical facilities were often separated from prisons. At Richmond prisons, ill soldiers were transported to facilities separate from prisons. Other Confederate facilities were hastily prepared with inadequate tent hospitals, such as those at Andersonville. In May 1864, Andersonville chief surgeon Isaiah H. White reported 209 small tents not suited for hospital use. With a capacity of 800, 1,020 were in the hospital tents with 2,665 sick in the stockade.[71] Dr. Joseph Jones, at Andersonville commander Captain Wirz's trial, described hospital conditions as, "The patients and attendants, near two thousand, are crowded, and are but poorly supplied with old and ragged tents. A large number of them are without any bunks in the tents, and lay upon the ground, oftentimes without even a blanket. No beds or straw appear to have been furnished."[72]

Conditions in the hospital tents of Belle Isle in 1864 were described by the US Sanitary Commission: "The bedding where the privates were confined by wounds was very dirty; the covering was entirely old, dirty quilts; the beds were offensive from the discharges from wounds and secretions of the body, and were entirely unfit to place a sick or wounded man on."[73] It should be noted that in the same report, the commission excuses any negative conditions and treatment in Union prisons and reports all were very satisfactory, dispelling any criticism received from the Confederacy.

However, Junius Browne, prisoner at Salisbury, wrote, "The hospitals were generally cold, always dirty and without ventilation, being little else than a protection from the weather." He further described

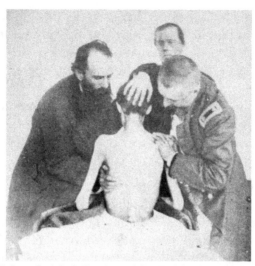

Examination of Private Isaiah G. Bowker of Co. B, 9th Maine Volunteers, at the U.S. General Hospital, Div. 1, Annapolis, after his release from Belle Isle Prison, Richmond, Virginia. (*Library of Congress*)

patients as, "Nearly all of them suffering from bowel complaints, and many too weak to move or be moved, one can imagine to what a state they were soon reduced."[74]

At the Union prison at Point Lookout, an inspection by US Sanitary Commission representative William F. Swalm was conducted in November 1863. He reported deplorable conditions, finding in the hospital "poor emaciated creatures" with chronic diarrhea sharing beds with smallpox victims. He judged the dispensary a "poor excuse for one." He described the hospital grounds, reporting, "they have not, according to looks, been policed for a very long time," and patients were "allowed to void their excrements in the most convenient place to them, regardless of the comfort to others."[75]

Smallpox was a constant threat and significant killer in both Union and Confederate prisons. The extent of smallpox at Camp Douglas was graphically described by prisoners Curtis R. Burke and Robert Bagby, the latter a nurse in the prison hospital.[76] Burke reported, "I learn that about two thirds of the prisoners sent to the smallpox hospital have died, and that there is about forty cases in the hospital now."[77] In November 1864, Bagby wrote, "There had been 35 new [smallpox] cases the day before increasing the number of patients to 255. From what I could learn, it was distressing to take care of them. A great many had no blankets and no bed. They were compelled to lie about on the floor like hogs."[78]

Prisoners and medical personnel feared smallpox. Most prisons provided separate hospital facilities for smallpox victims. Unfortunately, during smallpox epidemics, prisoners with smallpox remained with the general population because facilities were limited. This contributed to the continued spread of the disease. Significant smallpox epidemics were reported in many prisons, including at Rock Island, Illinois, and Point Lookout in late 1863 and early 1864.

Smallpox vaccine had been developed in 1796 by Edmond Jenner. Union military units and Confederate prisoners were routinely vaccinated against the disease. Even with the availability of vaccination against smallpox, the problem persisted. Frequently prisoners, as well as other soldiers, would refuse inoculation. Solon Hyde, Union prisoner at Danville Prison, indicated, "I would rather have taken the chances on smallpox than to open a suppurating sore, almost certain to follow vaccination in a system full of scurvy, and everything about having a tendency to foster gangrene. The entire virus I saw bore the U.S. mark and was mostly from Philadelphia."[79] Similarly, prisoner Curtis R. Burke at Camp Douglas in September 1864 wrote, "Our regiment was vaccinated and I washed mine off and squeezed it to keep it from taking. For I would rather run the risk of the smallpox than have the sore that some of them have on their arms." [80]

Military doctors, supplemented by civilian physicians, typically administered medical treatment to prisoners. Generally, these medical professionals did their best to serve prisoners. Captured physicians were often available to treat patients. Commonly, staffing, beds, and medications were insufficient to provide adequate treatment. The lack of medicine, especially in the Confederacy, and inadequate or insufficient facilities, made the job of treating prison maladies extremely difficult.

The Union blockade made medical support in the Confederacy more difficult. In July 1864, Andersonville prisoner and medical technician Solon Hyde observed, "The stock of drugs was meagre, consisting, in the main, of 'roots and herbs' packed by the Confederate Medical Dispensary at Macon, Georgia. The United States had so effectually blockaded the Southern ports that it was a difficult matter for them to get drugs that required chemical manipulation, all they had having either run the blockade or been captured from the 'Yanks.' Consequently, we had only a limited quantity of quinine, opium, mercurial preparations, etc., though what we had were generally good and bore the stamp of English manufacture."[81]

This limited medical treatment failed to recognize the risk to Confederate prisoners of a change in diet from pork and corn to beef and bread. Also, the rural upbringing of the average Confederate soldier produced little contact with large numbers of individuals or common diseases. Thus, these soldiers lacked natural immunity and were not able to fight off common communicable diseases, such as measles and mumps.

Union medical services were delivered at facilities designed to treat Union soldiers. In theory, treatment should have been better than Confederate treatment at the South's makeshift hospitals, but there is little evidence to support this. While the death rate at Union prisons was 3 percent less than that in Confederate prisons, it does not reflect that there was significantly better medical treatment for prisoners. On the contrary, the effective Union blockade resulted in many medicines not being available to Confederate wounded as well as Union prisoners.

Neither side could be proud of the quality of medical care provided to prisoners. Both sides should have been ashamed of the incidence of scurvy that could have been avoided with the simple distribution of fresh vegetables. It is impossible to explain why, at Camp Douglas, Colonel Hoffman in 1864 refused to allow sutlers to sell vegetables or why commander Colonel Benjamin Sweet did not spend available prison funds to provide vegetables that were readily available locally.[82]

The medical care in Civil War prisons was essentially the same as that provided to the Civil War field soldier. Disease, the number-one killer of prisoners in both Union and Confederate prisons, was comparable to the overall loss of life among the soldiers in combat. Primitive medical knowledge, inadequate hospital facilities, and medicine shortages contributed to this unfortunate reality. Victorian-era medicine did not offer care that properly addressed prisoner or combatant needs. As static facilities, most prison camps should have provided better care than mobile armies; however, lack of attention to the medical threats and indifference to prisoner welfare likely contributed to continuing ineffective medical care.

SANITARY CONDITIONS

Poor sanitary conditions in all Civil War prisons were significant causes of medical problems. The locations of camps such as Camp Douglas, Camp Morton, Point Lookout, Belle Isle, and other prisons on swampy soil and the fouling of the only water supply at Andersonville and Elmira created specific problems. Camp Douglas, as well as Belle Isle and other camps, were subject to flooding and standing water. Elmira was located on land below the level of the adjacent Chemung River.

In late October 1861, prisoner J. Lake Fitts, 2nd New Hampshire Volunteers, captured at Bull Run, was moved by train from Richmond to Salisbury where, "Our water here was furnished by two wells, One of them was very good, the other was what we called sulphur water, having a strong taste and smell of sulphur. The well of good water was soon exhausted, and the sulphur water soon became so low that only part of a bucket of muddy stuff could be obtained at a time."[83] Later, in 1864, Colonel Homer Sprague reported, "We procured water from a deep well on the [Salisbury] grounds. The supply was so scanty for the thousands of prisoners that it was always exhausted before sunrise."[84]

Water was also a significant problem at Fort Delaware. Originally the water supply came from collecting rainwater from roofs that filtered through sand, earth, gravel, and bricks. The quantity was insufficient as more and more prisoners arrived at the fort. A steam water boat then brought water from the Brandywine River. Unfortunately, this water was unfiltered and caused diarrhea and other sickness among the prisoners. In the summer of 1864, during a hot, dry period, when water was transferred from the delivery boat to storage tanks, dead fish, worms, rotted leaves, and other salty jellied masses were stirred up from the tank sediment.[85]

Human waste was a problem in nearly all camps. H. M. Davidson described 1862 unsanitary conditions at Smith Prison in Richmond:

> The privies were constructed in the Northeast corner of each room, without doors, and were entered through an open window. Water was furnished through pipes and faucets from the James river. The

stench from the privies, which came constantly into the room, together with the dampness caused by water drizzling from the wash
sink, and from the cups, into which it was drawn to be drank, and
our crowded state, filled the air with poison, and rendered our physical systems doubly susceptible of diseases and contagion.[86]

Later, sanitary conditions at Danville were described by Davidson as,
"The filth and stench arising from our rooms, pent up as we were like
cattle, with no means of egress, and more than half of us sick with that
scourge of the soldier—the chronic diarrhea—was beyond description."[87]

Upon arrival as a prisoner at Andersonville in July 1864, Solon
Hyde observed,

The waters of the creek, soon after passing the dead line, were made
to pass through a crib extending nearly across the enclosure. Here
were the sinks, and the water served to keep them clean, the only
provision for cleanliness or evidence of care in the whole outfit, and
I have often wondered how even this was thought of. Just above the
stockade on the west, near the north entrance, stood the cook-house,
a board shanty in which were a furnace and kettles for doing the
cooking, and an oven for baking our corn bread, which was done by
a detail of our own men. All the filth of this passed into the stream,
making the water so foul that it was not fit to drink. The stream also
received all the filth and wash from the Rebel camps and sinks.[88]

Open-slit trenches for toilet facilities, simple buckets, and improp-
erly closed latrines were common substitutes for sanitary toilet facilities in prisons. Failing to protect fresh water supplies and improper
handling of food and offal made the already serious sanitary conditions in camps much worse.

In the fall of 1863, The Union considered removing Confederate
prisoners from Camp Chase. The camp was considered to be a "present filthy location." Nothing, however, came of this suggestion.[89] At
Camp Douglas, an inspection by Dr. Humphrey of the Sanitary Commission in February 1863 recommended the camp be abandoned.[90]
In May 1863, comments included "deplorable conditions," "filth," "little drainage," and recommendations for improved sewage facilities.[91]
In October 1863, medical inspector M. Clark found drainage inadequate, policing neglected sinks with "no management," and the prison
was generally filthy. He did note that sewers were being installed.[92]

From the beginning, Camp Morton in Indianapolis was plagued by standing water and flooded conditions that added to health concerns for the Union soldiers stationed there as well as the Confederate prisoners. Prisoners called the small ditch that flooded during rain "the Potomac."[93]

Unsanitary conditions, exacerbated by delays in remediation, ignorance, and neglect, were major contributors to medical problems for prisoners. Overcrowding and poor selection of camp sites subjected Union and Confederate prisoners to significant health risks. Neither side ever adequately addressed sanitation problems of the camps.

BRUTAL GUARDS

There were many examples of mistreatment of prisoners. Worse, evidence of guards killing prisoners and administering inhumane punishment in Civil War prisons is not uncommon. The extent of this brutality, however, has been overstated and can be linked to the Lost Cause movement. There is no evidence of a conspiracy to kill or maim prisoners by either the Union or Confederate governments.

There is also evidence that Union colonel Hoffman and US Secretary of War Stanton were willing to support retaliation for Union prisoner mistreatment by carrying out the same against Confederate prisoners. In response to complaints of poor treatment by Confederate officers held at Camp Chase, Hoffman, in April 1863, supported Union guards' retribution for treatment of "our people." After reports of mistreatment of Union prisoners in Richmond, Secretary Stanton, in November 1863, directed US Commissioner for Exchange Ethan Allen Hitchcock "to use measures for precisely similar treatment toward all Confederate prisoners held by the United States."[94]

Union prisoner J. Lake Fitts, imprisoned in 1861 in Richmond's Pemberton tobacco factory, stated,

> We are in charge of the notorious Wirtz [Henry Wirz, later commander of Andersonville], the officer above him was Lieutenant Todd, a brother of Abraham Lincoln's wife [David H. Todd, Mary Todd Lincoln's half-brother]. Lieutenant Todd, when upon the street near our windows one day, overheard some conversation that did not suit him. He drew his sword and rushing upstairs, stabbed the first man he came across, wounding him so that he had to be removed to the hospital. 'Every d——d Yankee' he said. 'ought to be

served the same way." Later, Fitts reported, "I have no doubt it [shooting a prisoner] was done by order of Wirtz as he threatened to 'order the guard to shoot every 'dam Yankee' who looked out the window.[95]

An Andersonville guard, Private James E. Anderson, was so concerned about frequent shootings by his fellow guards that he wrote President Jefferson Davis: "We have many thoughtless boys here who think killing of a Yankee will make them great men. . . . Last Sabbath there were two shot in their tents at one shot."[96] There is no record of any response from the Confederate government.

In May 1865, Confederate prisoner Creed T. Davis at City Point reported, "The negro guard last night bayonetted a prisoner without the slightest provocation, killing him upon the spot, and shot at another man, but luckily missed his aim."[97] Negative comments about "negro" guards were common in writing by Confederate prisoners. It is likely that much of the criticism of these guards was prejudice-based.

In 1864, at Danville, Union prisoner Solon Hyde observed, "A large percentage of the Danville guards were men who did not value the life of a Yankee very highly, and seemed on the alert for a pretext to shed blood." He continued, "As an instance of their disregard of life, I may mention the following incident: Nearly opposite our building, on the west side, stood a small house occupied by some negro washerwomen, one of whom, while hanging out a washing, was deliberately shot at by a guard of No. 3, the ball breaking her arm. Several of our boys who were looking out of the windows at the time were witnesses of the whole affair, and saw nothing in the actions of the woman to provoke the act. It just seemed to be the leaven of the Devil working in them that had to have vent some way in the shedding of blood."[98]

Hyde also commented about guards who accompanied them in a move from Danville to Andersonville: "He [a guard] was very abusive to the boys, striking them or punching them with his gun if they did not move to suit his ideas. I also noticed the corporal (the one who had had charge of us in the corner) strike a man over the head with his ramrod simply because he happened to step a little out of line at one of our stopping-places."[99]

In 1864, Union captain Joseph Ferguson reported, "The Georgia militia guarding the Macon jail were vindictive and brutal, and their officers encouraged them in their savage acts. Promotion and furloughs were promised, and given, to those who would shoot, or kill a Yankee, All the officers."[100] Later, at Columbia, South Carolina, Ferguson noted, "On the morning of December first I was trying to kindle a fire with green wood to cook a pot of mush, when I was startled by the report of a rifle back of my hut. I jumped up and walked towards the imaginary dead-line and discovered that Lieutenant Turbayne, of the Sixty-sixth New York Volunteers, had been shot through the heart murdered by a friend called Williams, of Newbury Court-House, South Carolina. The soldier of the Union was shot whilst walking along a path that ran by the corner of a hut, but inside of the dead line. Along this path the captives had walked since their entry into prison, without fear or molestation, as it was their own ground."[101]

Colonel Homer Sprague reported this novel form of punishment at Danville in 1864, "We arrived at Danville at noon. A heavy rain began to fall. Having been two days without opportunity to wash, we were drenched for an hour or two by the sweet shower that seemed to pour from the open windows of heaven. When our thoughtful guards concluded that we were sufficiently cleansed and bleached, they sheltered us by putting us into coal cars, where the black dust was an inch deep."[102]

Prisoners John M. Copley and Curtis R. Burke at Camp Douglas each reported five specific guards who were known for excessive brutality.[103] Copley described these guards:

> The police guards within the inclosure of the prison were armed with large army pistols, loaded. The authority of each was absolute, and from it there was no appeal, at least, an appeal made by any of us would not have been heard by higher authority. Their duties were to patrol the prison grounds and barracks at all hours during the day and night; to see that all the rules and regulations of the prison were strictly carried out; that no plots or conspiracies were planned or organized among the prisoners to escape, and that the sanitary rules and regulations were rigidly executed. Quite a number of them were within the inclosure of the prison walls day and night.[104]

At Camp Douglas four of the most infamous police were known as the "Big Four" by prisoners. Prisoners Curtis Burke and John Copley both identified these four as the cruelest police who were responsible for administering the most brutal punishment.[105] While other

Confederate prisoners "riding the mule" at Camp Douglas. (*Library of Congress*)

guards were reported as reasonable, these four preyed, unsupervised, on Confederate prisoners. Inmates considered guard officers as responsible as the four policemen for mistreatment of prisoners.

Dr. R. Randolph Stevenson, chief confederate surgeon at Andersonville, reported, without indicating the source, that in the winter of 1863–1864 at Camp Douglas, "The prisoners in barrack No. 10 were ordered out and made to pull down their clothes and sit naked upon the ice. The crime committed was bespattering the spitbox too much. Sometimes men would be ordered out at night, and forced to lean over, without bending the knee, and touch the ground with the forefinger. This was termed 'pointing for grub.'"[106]

Much corporal punishment administered by guards was similar to punishment given to fellow soldiers. Riding the "mule" or "horse" was common. The mule or horse was similar to a sawhorse constructed of wood and often ten feet high or more. Offenders would be required to sit on the horse for hours. Especially egregious offenders would have weights attached to their feet while "riding" as additional punishment. Hanging by the thumbs, standing on barrels, and wearing signs of offenses were common punishments in both armies as well as for prisoners. Special punishment, such as squatting or sitting for long periods in inclement weather, was punishment often limited to prisoners.

In January 1865, Curtis Burke, at Camp Douglas, reported:

About midnight two patrol guards came in our barrack and caught one of the men sitting by one of the stoves smoking, and made him climb up on one of the rafters and act circus. He was sitting astraddle of the rafter to blow. After performing numerous feats, when I gave Henry a punch in the short ribs to wake him up to see the performance. I pointed to the actor and whispered to him to look and keep quiet. He looked rubbed his eyes and looked again and said "That is nothing but some body's old clothes hanging there." But he soon discovered his mistake as the guard ordered the performance to go on. Just then someone woke up and not knowing that a guard was in the house spit on the floor. The guard immediately ordered him out of his bunk and made him take the place of the man on the rafter who was glad enough to get off. The second actor performed about half an hour and was dismissed.[107]

At Camp Morton, prisoners were frequently required to march in place in deep snow for up to an hour. Guards there then reportedly beat prisoners for no reason with rolled up heavy rubber cloth.[108]

Not all guards were committed to violence and mistreating prisoners. Union prisoner W. H. Lightcap had an interesting discussion with Confederate guards while traveling to Columbus, Georgia. "We wish we had the pleasure and honor of wearing a blue suit like yours. I was astonished and asked, 'Do you mean it?' 'Yes, indeed we do.' 'How is it you are members of the Rebel army?' We could not help ourselves. We could not get away with our families to the north where we could enter the Federal service and were forced into the Rebel army, but no Union soldier was ever harmed by shots from our guns, for we always shoot high."[109] Lightcap also noted his treatment upon arrival at Andersonville:

We were ordered to strip to our skin, place our clothes in a pile to our right, with a double guard around us with orders to shoot the first man who moved a muscle. They searched every seam and pocket of our clothes and took everything, even pocket knives and tobacco, no matter how small, also photographs, which would be a source of comfort for the possessors to look at but of no value to them; every poncho, blanket or tent, if any were so unfortunate as to have them, and all the time cursing, damning and calling us vile names.[110]

Misuse of authority and inappropriate behavior was not limited to enlisted guards. Officers frequently demanded money and property from inmates. They also ignored the actions of guards who reported to them. Union lieutenant Cooper reported the following in his account of activities at Camp Oglethorpe: "We drew three or four days' rations at a time. These rations consisted of two ounces of bacon, half a pint of rice, a pint of corn meal, and a teaspoonful of salt a day per man; but when Capt. W. Kemp Tabb took command of the prison camp he at once cut these down one-third." [111]

Inappropriate actions by guards can be attributed, largely, to poor selection, poor training, and ineffective supervision. Had the North or South desired, both training and selection of guards could have been significantly improved. While the Confederacy had significant demands for frontline troops, there were sufficient noncombat men to provide adequate guards.

WEATHER CONDITIONS

Harsh weather conditions in the North contributed significantly to health problems of Confederate prisoners. Coupled with poor clothing and insufficient or lack of bedding material, cold temperatures caused a significant number of deaths. Diarists frequently commented on radically cold temperatures during incarceration; however, comments of minus twenty-five degrees were overstatements. A review of local temperature records shows that Civil War winters were statistically no worse than current weather.[112] In the South, hot weather also affected prisoners. Across prisons, cold and rain in camps with inadequate shelter in winter and summer increased sanitation and medical problems.

At the trial of Andersonville commander Captain Wirz, testimony included:

> From a temperature ranging during the summer up to near 150 Fahrenheit in the sun, as Dr. Thornburg tells you, during which there were many cases of sun-stroke, it fell in the winter to a temperature much below the freezing-point, nothing being left these miserable creatures with which to resist the inclemency of the weather but diseased and emaciated bodies, and ragged, worn-out clothing. Dr. Thornburg says that during the winter there was weather sufficiently severe to have frozen to death men with the scanty supplies these prisoners had, and in their emaciated condition; and Dr. Eice, after

stating that the prisoners were exposed more or less during the whole winter, says, I knew a great many to die there who I believed died from hunger and starvation, and from cold and exposure.[113]

While commanders had no control over the weather, providing prisoners proper clothing, shelter, and bedding was a command responsibility.

PHYSICAL CONDITION OF PRISONERS UPON ARRIVAL AT CAMPS
Many prisoners had been subjected to poor conditions in the battle areas. These conditions were exacerbated by improper treatment as they were moved to prison facilities.

For example, nearly thirteen thousand Confederates surrendered to Ulysses S. Grant at Fort Donelson on February 16, 1862, after over four days of fighting in cold, rainy, and snowy weather. Grant issued three-days of rations to prisoners and allowed them to take any personal equipment, except weapons, they could carry.[114] The men were then placed on unheated steamboats and sent north on the Cumberland River to the Ohio River and ports controlled by the North. Many were put on unheated Illinois Central rail cars at Cairo for a trip to Chicago and Camp Douglas. The prisoners arrived there between February 20 and 27 in freezing temperatures. Other prisoners were sent to Camp Butler, Camp Chase, and Alton Prison with the same delays and poor weather conditions. Camp Morton reported that more than half of the prisoners from Fort Donelson were in need of medical treatment. Some Fort Donelson wounded were sent to St. Louis, and later to prison camps.

John Copley was captured at the Battle of Franklin in Tennessee on November 30, 1864, and marched to Nashville in snow arriving December 1. Copley, who began with the Army of Tennessee march from Atlanta in mid-October, reported that the troops had abandoned much of their equipment including overcoats and extra uniforms. During the march to Franklin and then to Nashville Copley reported in his journal that the troops had little to eat, were poorly clothed, and were often barefoot. The prisoners were transported by rail boxcars from Nashville to Louisville on December 2. Other prisoners indicated that Confederate prisoners on the march from Franklin could be followed by the bloody footprints in the snow. After a night in Louisville, they marched to a depot and were loaded "on board a train of box cars and were packed in like beef cattle for shipment." The prisoners arrived at daylight, December 5, 1864, at Camp Douglas. They stood in snow for "several hours" while they were stripped and searched before being placed in barracks."[115] Similar stories of the poor condition and treatment of arriving Confederate prisoners were reported at Camp Morton.[116]

These two examples at the beginning and ending of the war were repeated time and again in the transportation of both Union and Confederate prisoners. Death statistics at many prison camps showed soldiers dying within days or weeks of arrival. In January 1863, Confederate soldiers captured at Arkansas Post (Fort Hindman, Arkansas) were reported in poor condition by guards accompanying them to St. Louis.[117] Upon arrival at Camp Douglas, the greatest death total in one month (378 in March 1864) was attributed to the condition of these Arkansas Post prisoners upon arrival less than ninety days before.[118]

The conditions of incarceration discussed in this chapter were common in prison camps on both sides and throughout the war and were the result of decisions made by the warring governments prior to and during the war. These conditions caused high death rates at several prisons. Andersonville, with a death rate of approximately 28 percent, is often used as the high mark. This death rate was exceeded by Salisbury Prison with a death rate of 34 percent (many prisoners were transferred to Salisbury from Andersonville). The Confederate death rate at Elmira, at 24 percent, was highest of the Union prisons. These rates were well above the estimated 12 percent for Confederate prisoners and 15 percent for Union prisoners.

The magnitude of prisoners' problems was amplified by the numbers of prisoners held—greater numbers than any war that followed: 431,400 prisoners were held during the Civil War (211,400 Union, 220,000 Confederate), compared to 147,227 Americans held as POWs from World War I through Vietnam. This great number of Civil War prisoners presented challenges to both North and South governments that were virtually impossible to resolve.

The following chapters discuss the five factors that help explain why these conditions continued throughout the Civil War.

CHAPTER 4

FACTOR ONE: LACK OF A STRATEGIC PLAN FOR HANDLING PRISONERS

istory of warfare to the 1860s established parole and exchange as the method of dealing with captured combatants. Based on this historic precedent, neither the governments of the North nor the South can be overly criticized for failure to develop a strategic plan for handling prisoners some other way. In the first place, both sides of the conflict were busy building armies. The Union had to develop a large volunteer army to supplement the nation's small standing army. The total US Army at the beginning of the Civil War was sixteen thousand with most personnel located west of the Mississippi River. Confederates had to develop a completely new army made up solely of volunteers led by a combination of volunteers and professional officers, many who left the service of the Union after secession. The only standing forces available to the South were ill-trained state militia units.

At the beginning of the war, parole and exchange was an acceptable strategy; however, the expansion of river and rail transportation, along with improved telegraph communications, presented field commanders with alternatives for handling prisoners—alternatives they were eager to consider with justification.

Parole of captured soldiers brought field commanders two problems. First, a mobile army has no capacity to feed, shelter, and guard large numbers of prisoners. Second, providing written parole took time that commanders could ill afford to lose. For example, in 1862, as a prelude to the Battle of Sharpsburg (Antietam), Union forces at Harper's Ferry surrendered to General "Stonewall" Jackson. It took the Confederates a full two days to process written parole to the twelve thousand Union prisoners. The process took these troops away from General Lee during the Sharpsburg battle. Confederate parole administrator General A. P. Hill arrived with his troops at Sharpsburg (after a seventeen-mile forced march) barely in time to support Lee's right flank at the end of the day's bloody battle.

Both Union and Confederate field commanders seized on the ability to move the prisoners away from the battlefield to become someone else's responsibility. Major General Rosecrans reporting to General U. S. Grant October 21, 1862: "My sending away paroled prisoners to Benton Barracks was in conformity with previous custom and in supposed accordance with your views of properly clearing them out of Corinth as rapidly as possible."[1]

CONFEDERATE RESPONSE TO THE LACK OF STRATEGIC PLAN FOR HANDLING PRISONERS

When, in July 1861, at the Battle of Manassas (Bull Run) in Virginia, the Confederates captured over 1,200 Union soldiers, the commanders were faced with managing these prisoners. For the young, mobile Confederate army, on-site parole was not practical. With rail transportation to Richmond available to remove the captives from the battlefield, prisoners were taken to Manassas Junction and loaded on the Virginia Central Railroad.

Without preparation or warning, the Jefferson Davis government was forced to assign responsibility for receiving the prisoners to Confederate brigadier general John Winder, provost marshal of Richmond.

General Winder's primary responsibility was policing Richmond, the new capital of the Confederacy. The fast-growing city attracted border state refugees, office seekers, and individuals of questionable character. General Winder had a full plate, before the additional requirement of managing newly arrived prisoners. He had little staff to manage the growing prison population. In July 1861, he complained to Adjutant General Cooper about high turnover of his staff, "These officers do not remain long enough to acquire sufficient knowledge of the details to assist me much."[2] He was not trained in prison management; based on his police background, he determined that the best place to house prisoners was in existing civilian jails and prisons. As available space was not, even initially, sufficient to meet the army's needs, Winder then acquired abandoned warehouses and factories in the Richmond area to be used to house prisoners. The use of these types of facilities would be repeated throughout the South for most of the war. Additionally, barren stockades were put to use. General Winder made most of his decisions for dealing with prisoners in response to each immediate crisis with little, if any, planning. As Roger Peckenpaugh observed in his book, *Captives in Blue*, "This makeshift approach would prove to be the general precedent for Southern prison policy for the rest of the war."[3]

The warehouses and factories had significant problems in meeting the barest of needs of the prisoners. There were no toilet facilities; the solutions ranged from using simple buckets in corners to outside latrines. Fresh water was rarely available in the buildings, requiring delivering water to the sites. The factories and warehouses frequently lacked adequate ventilation, heat, and light.

Early in the war most prisoners remained in Richmond. In the short term, Richmond facilities were sufficient to meet the space needs to house prisoners; they were not intended to house prisoners long term. In late 1861, a few facilities opened in North and South Carolina and outside Richmond in Virginia. As prisoners were moved outside Richmond, lack of planning was even more evident. For example, prisoners being moved to Castle Pickney, SC, were forced to be housed in local prisons until Castle Pickney was available to handle prisoners.[4]

General Winder would continue to be responsible for prisoners as an additional duty to his provost marshal responsibilities; however, his duties and responsibilities were never clearly set forth in writing. Rather, they were word-of-mouth and spread over a variety of orders and other written communications. Even though Confederate prison facilities expanded beyond Richmond he was not named as commissary of prisoners until November 1864. As provost marshal, he had limited influence over quartermaster and other logistic support for prisons and prisoners outside of Richmond. The lack of authority and influence over resources plagued General Winder and the Confederacy prison system throughout the war. This organization confusion in the Confederacy was evident from the beginning and continued throughout the war.[5]

With the problems at Andersonville, General Winder on July 25, 1864, wrote Adjutant General Samuel Cooper, "There are 29,400 prisoners, 2,650 troops, 500 negroes and other laborers and not a ration at the post." After forwarding General Winder's concerns to Commissary General Lucius B. Northrop, General Northrop informed Adjutant General Cooper that Winder had nothing to do with feeding prisoners and that it was the concern of the commissary general. He indicated the adjutant general was responsible for custody, and Winder, if he had concerns, should have contacted him. Thus, according to General Northrup, General Winder had little, if any, responsibility for prisons and prisoners.

As resources were stretched by increased prisoner population and as Union military pressure increased, the Confederacy was forced to establish more prisons. Often these prisons had a short life because, increasingly, all Confederate resources were needed to fight the battles of the war and the encroaching Union army. Infamous Andersonville was in operation only fourteen months before Union military pressure forced the Confederates to move the prisoners as Union forces advanced into Georgia.

The need for Andersonville and other remote prisons was summarized by Ambrose Spencer:

> The accumulation of prisoners of war at Richmond and Salisbury was so great as to cause serious inconvenience to the rebel authorities, congregated as the prisoners were at and near the centre of their military operations at one extremity of the Confederacy, exposed to recapture, and requiring the detail of a large force for their safe keeping. The greatest disadvantage arising from the concentration of so many thousand prisoners at the seat of the Confederate government was the consumption of provisions destined for their army, together with the difficulty of transporting immense stores to that point, over single lines of roads with insufficient capacities, and for a thousand miles from the region where they were produced. These roads were liable to be broken, as they ultimately were, by the Union

Confederate brigadier general John Winder, left, provost marshal of Richmond, and Brigadier General Montgomery Meigs, right, quartermaster general of the US Army. (*Library of Congress*)

forces, and thus the means of provisioning their army, as well as the prisoners, be entirely cut off. Under these circumstances, it was determined to establish military prisons at points more remote from the theatre of war.[6]

The Confederacy never adequately documented or consistently communicated the guidelines for prisoner treatment. Command responsibility for prisoners was never adequately documented by the Confederacy. Information was disseminated in a variety of individual unit orders and directives that were never centralized. "Rules and Regulation of the C.S. Military Prisons" (See Appendix VI) was published in 1863. This document provided some detailed requirements for prison commanders and guards but provided little direction on the treatment of prisoners.

Confederate response to the need to house, feed, and clothe prisoners of war was, at best, reactionary. General Winder was never given proper support. His management of the prison system was makeshift from the beginning, resulting in inadequate treatment of prisoners. The magnitude of the initial task and immediate crises left little time to consider long-term incarceration of prisoners.

UNION RESPONSE TO THE LACK OF STRATEGIC PLAN

The first discussion of captured combatants in the Union army was in a telegram from Major General George B. McClellan on July 13,

1861, to the War Department. He inquired after capturing six hundred officers and men in Rich Mountain, West Virginia, "The question is an embarrassing one. Please give me immediate instructions by telegraph as to the disposition to be made of officers and men taken as prisoners of war."

In response that same day, the War Department issued General Order 44 directing McClellan to release the prisoners on parole after they sign an oath of allegiance to the United States.[7] On July 14, Major General Winfield Scott clarified the oath to be limited to not taking up arms against the Union.[8] Earlier, on June 12, Brigadier General Montgomery Meigs, who had been appointed quartermaster general of the US Army on May 15, identified the impending need for handling Confederate captives. He wrote Secretary of War Simon Cameron that, "The conflict now commenced it is likely to be expected that the United States will have to take care of a large number of prisoners of war."[9]

In view of the history of captives in earlier wars, Meigs was unusually perceptive of the changing conditions in the Civil War. He was given ultimate responsibility for Confederate prisoners held by the Union. Assigned by Secretary of War Stanton and reporting to General Meigs, Lieutenant Colonel William Hoffman (later promoted to colonel and brevet brigadier general, referred to as Colonel Hoffman throughout this book) was appointed commissary of prisoners in October 1861, with his duties provided in writing in June 1862. Colonel Hoffman's responsibilities were specific:

GENERAL ORDERS, WAR DEPT., ADJT. GENERALS OFFICE, No. 67.
Washington, June 17, 1862.
"The supervision of prisoners of war sent by generals commanding in the field to posts or camps prepared for their reception is placed entirely under Col. William Hoffman, Third Infantry, commissary general of prisoners, who is subject only to the orders of the War Department. All matters in relation to prisoners will pass through him.

He will establish regulations for issuing clothing to prisoners, and will direct the manner in which all funds arising from the saving of rations at prison hospitals or otherwise shall be accounted for and disbursed by the regular disbursing officers of the departments in providing under existing regulations such articles as may be absolutely necessary for the welfare of the prisoners.

He will select positions for camps for prisoners (or prison camps) and will cause plans and estimates for necessary buildings to be prepared and submitted to the Quartermaster-General upon whose approval they will be erected by the officers of the Quartermasters Department.

He will if practicable visit the several prison camps once a month.

Loyal citizens who may be found among the prisoners of war confined on false accusations or through mistake may lay their cases before the commissary-general of prisoners, who will submit them to the Adjutant-General.

The commissary-general of prisoners is authorized to grant paroles to prisoners on the recommendation of the medical officer attending the prison in case of extreme illness but under no other circumstances.

By order of the Secretary of War.[10]

Even after the appointment of Colonel Hoffman, other commanders often confused matters by directing prison commanders in their area of responsibility. For example, Major General H. W. Halleck, commander of the Department of the Mississippi, on February 2, 1862, gave specific instruction to Colonel S. Burbank, commander in Alton, Illinois, on the operations of the Alton Prison. His instructions were specific to individual officer responsibilities at the prison, daily prisoner activities, burial of the dead, and required monthly reports to Halleck.[11] Likewise, Colonel Thomas Grant, provost marshal of St. Louis, interfered with the duties of the commander of Alton, requiring interaction by Colonel Hoffman on October 13, 1862.[12] These interferences by other offices with Colonel Hoffman's responsibilities would be evident throughout the war.

While the Union did not have a specific strategic plan for managing prisoners, with Meigs and Hoffman they clearly organized the army to address the problem. This proved to be effective for providing leadership for Union management of prisons. Their frugal approach to prisons, however, would mitigate the effectiveness of their management guidelines by providing inadequate housing, food, and medical care.

General Meigs and Colonel Hoffman were both concerned about financial expenditures throughout their tenure. Their close control of finances would have an adverse effect on improvements and development of prison facilities in the Union. For example, Colonel Hoffman, in a letter to General Meigs dated March 17, 1862, described his ideas on housing prisoners at Fort Delaware in great detail. He especially commented on how to accomplish the development as economically as possible, including "all rough boards without batting, without ceilings and without shingles."[13]

A centralized directive, General Order 100, was published over the signature of President Lincoln in April 1863 (see Appendix V). This order contained broad guidelines but nominal information on the treatment of prisoners (see Section III of General Order 100). It remained in effect throughout the war. General Order 100 was written by Francis Lieber and became the basis for The Hague Conference of 1899 for a strategic outline for the treatment of prisoners of war.

Battles in the east resulted in early development of facilities for prisoners in New York State, for example Fort Wood and Castle Williams. While used through most of the war, they were relatively small. Facilities at Point Lookout in 1863 and Fort Delaware in mid-1862 were developed as additional space was required. Planned to initially handle relatively few prisoners, Point Lookout soon became the largest prison in the Union system. The surrender by Confederates to General U. S. Grant of Fort Donelson in February 1862 created the need for significant prison facilities in the west, as that surrender gave General Grant nearly 12,500 prisoners to administer. Grant used the river system to the north and rail transportation to Union areas to move prisoners away from the war. After that move, these prisoners were no longer Grant's problem and became the headache of General Henry Halleck, Union commander of the Department of Missouri, who was given responsibility for identifying locations for the Confederate prisoners captured at Fort Donelson. He implemented three criteria for Union prisons:

> They needed to be far enough away from the battle areas to discourage raids to free prisoners.
> They should be on good transportation from the battle zone.
> They should be near population centers to provide logistic support.

Mustering in facilities in Chicago and Springfield, Illinois, Indianapolis, and Columbus, Ohio, met those criteria. Camp Douglas, Camp Butler, Camp Morton, and Camp Chase were selected. They

Camp Chase, Ohio, in 1864. (*National Archives*)

were supplemented by existing jails, such as Alton, Illinois, and existing military facilities at Rock Island, Illinois. These facilities offered barracks, mess facilities, and other logistic support and were not 100 percent occupied by Union troops. To receive prisoners, improvements of fencing and segregation of prisoners from Union forces was needed, as was identification and assignment of guards.

With this model, using existing facilities throughout the North became the standard for Union prisons. Other camps, including Fort Delaware and Point Lookout, were prison camps directly associated with existing military fort and medical facilities.

After the effective organization and selection of existing facilities as Union prisons, responsibility between the US and state governments needed to be resolved. At Camp Douglas, reporting responsibility was unclear. Colonel Hoffman sent a telegram to Captain Joseph A. Potter, assistant quartermaster, Camp Douglas, on February 24, 1862, after Potter inquired into whether he or the state held responsibility to manage Camp Douglas. "The prisoners are the prisoners of the United States!" Hoffman declared. "The supplies to be issued are the property of the United States. You are an officer of the United States. The State of Illinois has no more right to give you orders than the State of Massachusetts. State Authorities have no right to give orders to an officer of the United States."[14]

One prison, Johnson's Island on Lake Erie near Sandusky, Ohio, was specifically planned by Colonel Hoffman. Hoffman established this prison for Confederate officers as the standard for Union prisons. While subject to severe weather, Johnson's Island demonstrated effective planning and construction and suffered low mortality. Colonel Hoffman assigned the 128th Regiment, Ohio Volunteers, who became known as "Hoffman's Battalion" as guards. Hoffman demanded that these guards be drilled to a "perfect state of discipline" before they arrived and practice mounting the guard daily.[15] This emphasis on guard quality was extremely unusual in either the North or South.

Confederate prisoner Captain W. A. Urban described Johnson's Island in June 1863: "Upon first sight, the island had quite a prepossessing appearance, being slightly sloped, having a nice sward of green grass, with here and there a stately shade tree. The cottages, offices and barracks were neat and clean, and, on the opposite side from where we landed, a beautiful forest made the whole look quite genial. The garrison consisted of "Hoffman's Battalion," which had been on duty there since the first existence of the institution. "They were all dressed in the full uniform authorized by army regulations, and formed quite a contrast to soldiers in active service."[16]

Prisoner Henry Shepard found conditions at Johnson's Island less than satisfactory. In addition to inadequate and poor-quality food, he noted, "During the winter of 1863-64, I was confined in one room with seventy other Confederates. The building was not sealed, but simply weather-boarded. It afforded most inadequate protection against the cold or snow, which at times beat in upon my bunk with pitiless severity. The room was provided with one antiquated stove to preserve 70 men from intense suffering when the thermometer stood at fifteen and twenty degrees below zero."[17]

Facilities at Camp Douglas, assigned to receive Ft. Donelson captives, were not prepared. In Chicago, Mayor John Rumsey complained that seven thousand Confederate prisoners would endanger the city and that the Union's small garrison would be unable to adequately guard the prisoners. He wired General Halleck on February

21, 1862, that "our best citizens are in great alarm for fear that the prisoners will break though and burn the city." Halleck replied, "It is a great pity if Chicago cannot guard them unarmed for a few days. No troops can be spared from here for that purpose at present."[18] Chicago police supplemented by volunteer constables were pressed into service to assist the army with guarding the prisoners. These special police remained at the camp until February 27.

CONCLUSION

While neither the Union nor Confederate governments developed strategic plans for handling prisoners of war, both reacted quickly to the necessity to provide facilities for prisoners.

The Union reaction was better organized, identifying and assigning officers to be responsible and selecting existing facilities for a majority of their prisons. The duties and responsibilities of Brigadier General Montgomery Meigs, quartermaster general, and Colonel William Hoffman, commissary of prisoners, were clear and in writing. The selection and adaptation of existing facilities as prisons would continue through the war.

The Confederacy was less organized and provided very little information or direction to field commanders on the management of prisoners. Provost Marshal brigadier general John Winder was selected to manage the prisons. His location and experience in Richmond caused him to order the selection of jail facilities as primary housing for captured Union prisoners. Quickly overwhelmed by the number of prisoners, Winder reacted by commandeering existing abandoned warehouses and factories. His action began the continued pattern of selecting these facilities when available throughout the Confederacy. This disorganized structure and reactionary approach by the South resulted in poor planning throughout the war.

The lack of a strategic plan for the management of prisoners significantly contributed to the extreme conditions in Civil War prisons. Based on historic precedent and pressing military needs, it is understandable that military leaders placed a low to nonexistent priority on providing a plan. However, early experience with prisoners demonstrated the practical and humane need for a comprehensive plan. However, neither side met this need.

While the Union was better organized, the preference by both the political and military leaders of the North and South was parole and exchange as the preferred method of handling prisoners. All, except perhaps General Meigs, failed to appreciate the tactical and technological changes that affected movement of troops and supplies on the battlefield. These forces made parole and exchange virtually unworkable in the field, thus feeding into the ad hoc development of the inadequate and often inhumane prison systems in both the North and South.

Had there been a strategic plan, both the North and the South could have codified policies and procedures for the conduct of prisoners and prisons. Special facilities could have been prepared to receive and hold prisoners at costs that would have been less in the North. The South could have avoided major movement of prisoners during the war by developing prisons deeper in the South. A strategic plan by the Confederates could have consolidated and reduced the number of prisons, allowing fewer and more senior officers to command larger facilities. Creation of a cadre of officers and guards to operate the prisons would have provided adequate protection to the populous where prisons were located and more efficient, consistent treatment of prisoners.

The next factor creating significant problems in prisoner management for both the Union and the Confederacy was a lack of a plan for the long-term incarceration of prisoners.

CHAPTER 5

FACTOR TWO: INADEQUATE PLANS FOR LONG-TERM INCARCERATION

The historic concept of parole and exchange continued to plague both governments throughout the war as prisoners continued to be captured and held. In June 1862, the Dix–Hill Cartel (see Appendix IV) was delivered to manage the parole and exchange of prisoners. This cartel did not address the ongoing treatment of held prisoners, only the mechanics of exchange and parole.

The most significant provision of the Dix–Hill Cartel was Article 4, which stated that captured prisoners would be paroled within ten days of capture. Processing paroles to meet this provision was not practical for mobile armies. The capture of Union forces at Harper's Ferry was not tactically convenient and became time consuming for the mobile Confederate forces there. On the other hand, the more than twelve thousand Confederates who surrendered at Vicksburg on July 4, 1863, could be paroled because General Grant's army was stationary and could process thousands of paroles in place.

Technical and tactical considerations permitted armies to remove prisoners from the battlefield and deliver them to the rear quickly and efficiently. Once prisoners could then be moved by rail and river transportation systems, they would become the responsibility of some other command. However, even with good transportation, the Dix–Hill goal of parole in ten days was impossible for either side.

CONFEDERATE RESPONSE TO THE LACK OF PLANS FOR LONG-TERM IN-CARCERATION

As Confederate battle successes continued, the Union prisoner count increased. When Richmond-area facilities were pressed to exhaustion, General Winder was forced to develop facilities outside. Converted buildings in Cahaba, Alabama, and in Castle Thunder and Danville, Virginia, were developed in late 1862 and 1863. The warehouse used as a prison at Cahaba in 1864 had lacked a roof or floor since 1861. In spite of this, Union prisoners were housed in this facility.[1]

As these types of facilities became more difficult to obtain, barren stockade facilities such as Belle Isle, Camp Ford, Salisbury, and later Andersonville were pressed into service.

A Union report on Libby Prison on November 26, 1863, and sent to the president, contained the following facts: "About one thousand officers of all grades, and from both branches of the service, are confined in Libby prison, whose walls are unplastered, thus open to the full sweep of the winter winds, or closed with boards rendering the place dark, dreary, and loathsome in the extreme. None of the private soldiers are furnished with bedding of any kind."[2]

The development of Confederate prisons outside Richmond was a problem for General Winder who continued to have primary responsibility as provost marshal of Richmond. With little logistic support, the new facilities often failed to meet even the minimum Confederate standards for prisoner treatment. Winder's problems were increased as Union forces advanced. From late 1863 and early 1864, prisoners were moved from facility to facility to avoid repatriation by Union forces. This placed additional pressure on the limited resources of the Confederacy. Little effort could be devoted to improving conditions of Union prisoners. Prisoner Solon Hyde described his transfer from Richmond's Libby and Pemberton Prisons to Danville and later to Andersonville by a variety of rail trips starting in late 1863, ultimately arriving at Andersonville on July 5, 1864.[3]

Andersonville was the only Confederate prison that was specifically planned. In November 1863, Confederate secretary of war James A. Sheldon ordered Captain W. Sidney Winder to consult with Georgia governor Joseph Brown and General Howell Cobb to select a prison site near Americus or Fort Valley. After several sites were rejected because of local opposition, Andersonville was selected.[4] Unfortunately, the planning and execution was insufficient and Andersonville became a notorious anomaly among Confederate prisons. Poor planning, inadequate facilities, overcrowding, and insufficient logistic support doomed Andersonville to failure.

The South used the lack of construction material as an excuse to not provide barracks for prisoners at Andersonville. The real problem wasn't lack of material; it was the cost of the material that was readily available. Local sawmills refused to provide necessary lumber at the payment rates established by the Confederacy.[5] Prisoner Robert Kellogg, upon arriving at Andersonville, observed, "The country about our camp was gently undulating, and not far from us were large pine forests, that evidently had not rang to the woodman's axe for a long tune, if ever."[6] There is no reasonable explanation why prisoner work parties were not permitted to cut lumber from the surrounding area. Andersonville became the essence of mistreatment of prisoners with the highest number (12,919) of deaths among all Civil War prisons.

In 1864, Union prisoner W. F. Lyon described his arrival at Andersonville: "We had been a week on the road since our capture, and were hungry and tired, consequently the thoughts uppermost in our minds were of rest and something to eat. We passed through the gate like 'dumb driven cattle' and we were treated by our keepers very much like cattle. No provision had been made for our reception. No place had been assigned for this body of 600 men, so each man must look out for himself."[7]

Conditions at Andersonville were so bad that Union lieutenant Ferguson commented in his journal,

> J. Nelson Clarke testified that he was taken as prisoner to Andersonville about the 28th of May, 1864, and confirmed the previous evidence as to the crowded and filthy condition of the stockade, the sufferings of the prisoners, the coarse, dirty and insufficient amount of rations, &c. In August of last year he counted one hundred and eighty-four dead men in the stockade. The witness mentioned the case of an insane soldier who wandered up and down by the stream, refusing to wear clothes, and who had not sense enough to know that he must cook his rations, and who ended his life by suicide.[8]

In October 1863, Lieutenant A. C. Roach, while a prisoner at Camp Sorghum (a barren stockade) in Columbia, South Carolina, reported with pride, "we had built a city that could boast as many styles of architecture as Gotham itself. Axes, spades and hatchets, were bought at enormous prices from the rebel guards, and of our scant allowance of wood for fuel, we saved out the best building timber of which frames were made, and covered with dirt and leaves."[9]

The Confederate haphazard approach to the development of a prison system reflected the total lack of a comprehensive plan for long-term incarceration of prisoners. Union prisoner Henry Eby, upon return to Belle Isle Prison in February 1864 after being a prisoner there in early 1863, noted conditions were unchanged or even worse.[10]

UNION RESPONSE TO THE LACK OF PLANS FOR LONG-TERM INCARCERATION

While the US prison structure was well organized, conflicts had plagued Union prison camps since the beginning. General Meigs and Colonel Hoffman were notorious for their frugal approach. Long term, the ten-day provisions of the Dix–Hill Cartel and the lack of a plan for long-term incarceration gave Union leadership an excuse to defer maintenance and improvements to prison facilities based on the response that Confederate prisoners would be housed for only a short time and then exchanged. Deferral of construction of a sewer and increasing water facilities from a three-inch pipe to six inches at Camp Douglas was a typical example of their short-sighted approach. On June 17, 1862, General Meigs informed Colonel Hoffman that the improvements were "expensive, not to say extravagant," and could not be done. He further required prisoner labor to complete building improvements.[11] When these improvements were completed, it was an example of too little too late.[12]

Responding to demand for additional space to relieve overcrowding at other prisons, especially Point Lookout, General Hoffman, on May 19, 1864, ordered Elmira commander Lieutenant Colonel Seth Eastman to prepare to receive prisoners.[13] Within days, foul sinks located near Foster's Pond at the Elmira location caused significant sanitation problems.[14] Later, when Colonel Benjamin Tracey planned to drain Foster's Pond, he considered it "a festering mass of corruption, impregnating the entire atmosphere of the camp with its pestilential odor, night and day." Hoffman supported Tracey's plan but complained about cost.[15] These problems would plague Elmira throughout the remainder of the prison's existence.

At Elmira Prison, Colonel Hoffman, early in 1864, refused to allow construction of barracks to reduce the use of tents for shelter. By fall of that year, five thousand prisoners were living outdoors. In October, Hoffman granted approval for the construction.[16]

Elmira was an existing mustering in camp for the Union, similar to a number of other camps converted to prison facilities. Colonel Hoffman, General Meigs, and Secretary Stanton understood the errors made and the resulting problems at the other facilities, which had been in existence since 1862. Even with this knowledge, Union leadership failed to identify and compensate for known potential problems at Elmira.

Colonel Hoffman continued his miserly approach when, in 1864, Union Colonel A. J. Johnson, commander at Rock Island, requested payment of forty cents per day for prisoner laborers. Hoffman approved ten cents for mechanics and five cents for laborers.[17] At Fort Delaware, to save money, Colonel Hoffman ordered that new barracks be erected without proper foundations. After they were occupied, Brigadier General Albin Schoepf reported, "In some places they have sunk nearly a foot."[18]

Even with the thrift of General Meigs and Colonel Hoffman and as ineffective as the system was, prison operations were a significant expense to the Union. In 1865, Elmira had the highest annual maintenance cost at $165,250, followed by Camp Douglas at $93,995. Camp Chase's costs were $52,134, Point Lookout $42,436, with Fort Delaware at $30,964. Twenty-seven camps under Hoffman's control spent $489,876.29 in 1865.[19] Costs to the Confederacy are not available; however, they were probably below those of the Union.

In addition to the specific responsibilities assigned to him in June 1862 by General Order 67, Colonel Hoffman petitioned Secretary of War Stanton for additional authority in April 1864 over departmental commanders (who outranked him) on matters relating to prison management. This included reporting, transportation assistance, and guards. He requested that guards provided by department commanders should not be withdrawn or reassigned without Colonel Hoffman's approval. On May 3, 1864, General Order 190 was published, spelling out the responsibilities of department commanders to Colonel Hoffman.[20]

Certainly, the Union failed to understand the long-term nature of incarceration during the war; however, General Meigs and Colonel Hoffman made things worse with their extremely frugal approach to prisons and prisoners. Only after the suspension of prisoner exchange in mid-1863 did the Union begin to address the needs of long-term prisoner incarceration. Then it was too little too late.

CONCLUSION

Using the provisions of the Dix–Hill Cartel as justification, the Union deferred improvements to prisons. As parole and exchange proved ineffective and, ultimately, was suspended, the Union prison system was never able to catch up.

With few resources and a mobile army, Confederate leadership had little time or interest in providing more than the bare minimum facilities in prisons. Military pressures and unanticipated overcrowding of Confederate prisons left little or no time or resources to develop a comprehensive plan for ongoing incarceration. Confederate general Winder had little alternative but to jump from problem to problem. The South's management of prisons continued to operate in a makeshift, disorganized manner. Leadership was unfocused and overextended, resulting in the chaotic treatment of prisoners.

This factor of no plan for long-term incarceration resulted in both Union and Confederate prison conditions that were never properly addressed during the war. Leadership on both sides failed to fully understand or appreciate problems related to prisons. Had either side acknowledged or planned for long-term incarceration, prisoner care would have been improved. The North could have avoided the deferral of improvements to facilities and the South the continual opening and closing of their facilities. It was clear early in the war that parole and exchange was not effective and the ten-day provision of the Dix–Hill Cartel was unworkable. Yet, neither side acknowledged this fact nor acted. Only after the suspension of parole in mid-1863 did both governments begin to accept reality.

Lack of planning led to the next factor that neither the Union nor the Confederacy appropriately addressed: poor selection and training of camp command.

CHAPTER 6

FACTOR THREE:
POOR SELECTION AND
TRAINING OF CAMP COMMAND

Both the Union and Confederacy selected prison camp commanders based on immediate availability rather than on qualifications. Neither side provided any training for camp commanders on their duties of prison management. On June 29, 1862, Colonel Joseph Tucker (the original commander of Camp Douglas in September 1861), when reassigned as the third Camp Douglas commander on June 19, 1862, required detailed instructions from Colonel Hoffman on his duties as commander.[1] This requirement for individual written instructions was typical during the war, as both sides lacked written orders. In spite of some written policies and procedures, commanders depended situation by situation upon specific instructions from either General Winder or Colonel Hoffman.

All prison camp commanders were faced with situations unknown to them and not in keeping with their military training, experience, or expectations. Officers expected subordinates to respect their position and rank. Unlike the commander's subordinates, prisoners showed little respect for the commander's position or rank. Quite frequently, prisoners treated commanders and other prison officers with disdain, refusing to follow orders and consistently challenging authority. This frustrated prison commanders and likely contributed to their mistreatment of prisoners.

CONFEDERATE RESPONSE TO SELECTION AND TRAINING OF CAMP COMMAND

Confederate general Winder received prisoners with little prior notice after the first Battle of Manassas, Virginia (Bull Run). After selecting existing jails and then abandoned warehouses and factories, the Confederacy faced appointing a commander for each of these small facilities. Junior officers were usually selected and made camp commanders, reporting directly to General Winder. These Confederate captains and lieutenants had no experience in handling prisoners and limited experience in basic military duties. Most of these officers were from local militia or state units. Winder had no organization to provide training or supervision of commanders; he was the organization himself. Typical of command, Belle Isle in late 1863 was commanded by Lieutenant Virginius Bossieux, "a rather young and gallant looking fellow," according to prisoner J. Osborn Colburn. Union soldier Colburn indicated the lieutenant was also "very cruel" when angered.[2]

John Urban, prisoner at a Florence, South Carolina, prison described the camp commanding officer: "The officer in charge of this prison was one Lieutenant Barrett, one of the most cowardly and brutal wretches that ever lived, and a fit companion for the brutal Dutch Captain Wirz and cowardly Davis. This Lieutenant Barrett frequently came into prison and fired a pistol over the heads of the prisoners, to see them dodge around to get away, and their fright appeared to give him intense delight."[3]

Captain Wirz, later at Andersonville, was reported to have said, "I am of more use to the Confederate Government than General Lee and his army, for I kill more d___d Yankees."[4]

Prisoner Willard W. Glazier characterized the commander of Libby Prison, "The commandant of the prison is Maj. Thomas P. Turner, of the C.S.A. He was formerly a student at West Point; but it is generally understood among the prisoners that he was expelled from that school for forgery. He was subsequently made captain in the Rebel service, and, for efficiency as a great Yankee destroyer, has recently been promoted to the rank of major."[5]

There were reports of frequent telegraphic communications by Colonel Hoffman and camp commanders of Union prisons in the official record. By contrast, General Winder's similar contacts with his commanders were conspicuously absent in the official record.

With a lack of command structure, the camp commanders were often left to communicate their requests directly to support units such as engineers and quartermasters. With only junior status, these Confederate officers would have little influence in obtaining support. In addition, not all commanders had authority over guard forces. Frequently guard units were commanded by officers of equal or greater rank than the camp commander.

As the war progressed, the Confederacy perpetuated this organization of camp command mostly with junior officers. With war demand high for officers in combat, prison commanders became even less experienced or were those who were deemed unfit for combat. While the North organized wounded and other officers and men unfit for field service into the Invalid Corps, the South had no such official organization to draw on for prison management. Confederate prison camp commanders were unprepared for their responsibilities and ineffective in providing for the care of their prisoners. This situation was known to Confederate leadership, but they took no action to correct these deficiencies.

UNION RESPONSE TO SELECTION AND TRAINING OF CAMP COMMAND

The Union Army's decision to use existing mustering in camps as primary prisons resulted in fewer, larger facilities for holding prisoners with more senior officers (colonels or brigadier generals) selected to command most of the camps. Through early 1863, most of these officers were commanders of units mustering in at the location where prisoners were held. These combat commanders had little desire to also act as prison camp commanders. Their primary goal was to complete mustering in a regiment and immediately move to the war zone. Thus, turnover became a problem at Union prisons. For example, in the three and a half years Camp Douglas held prisoners, there were twelve command changes with nine different commanders, plus three junior officers in command when the prison population was reduced as a result of prisoner exchanges.[6]

Likewise, at Point Lookout, there were four commanders in less than two years. The longest tenure at Point Lookout was Brigadier

General James Barnes who served for eleven months. Other commanders served for less than five months.[7] Camp Morton was also subject to high turnover until Colonel Ambrose A. Stevens arrived to serve as commander from October 1863 until the end of the war.[8]

At Camp Douglas, in August 1863, when nearly all prisoners had been paroled, Captain J. S. Putnam was placed in charge. On August 13, 1863, he notified Colonel Hoffman that the camp "was in good condition and could accommodate 8,000 prisoners. I have 125 guards."[9] Union captain J. A. Potter, the experienced camp quartermaster, immediately wired Colonel Hoffman, "I have just learned that you have been told that Camp Douglas could accommodate 8,000. This is in error. Six thousand including the guards is the utmost limit and then they will be crowded. Please have a commandant sent; also a good officer."[10] This demonstrates the lack of skill of the caretaker officers and Colonel Hoffman's ongoing lack of attention to details of this nature.

Turnover of Union commanders resulted in poor communications with Colonel Hoffman on prison needs. By the time a commander determined needs and communicated them to Colonel Hoffman, the commander was replaced. The new commander began a period of identifying needs only to be transferred to the war zone. Colonel Hoffman could then justify inaction since needs were not efficiently communicated and followed up by camp commanders.

Senior command was aware of the high turnover and its effect on prison operations. Colonel Hoffman, in February 1862, wrote the Ohio governor of Camp Chase, "Much embarrassment results from the frequent changes of the officers in charge of the (Camp Chase) prisoners."[11] Hoffman also commented on command at Camp Douglas. In May 1863, he reported to Secretary Stanton, "It is almost impossible to have instructions carried out at Camp Douglas because of the frequent changes of commanders."[12] It is clear that Colonel Hoffman understood the problems with officer turnover; yet, until mid-1863, he took no action to correct the situation.

When senior officers were assigned as prison camp commanders, they had the experience and rank to influence support organizations to respond to their demands. A general or colonel could pull rank effectively when demanding support. However, high commander turnover mitigated this advantage. Commonly, unqualified officers were given discretionary funds including savings from food purchases and funds held for prisoners who had died. Often, they did not know how and on what they were authorized to expend these funds.[13]

In 1863, as the Invalid Corps (later renamed the Veteran Reserve Corps) came into existence, these units and officers took greater responsibility as cadre for Union prisons. They increased continuity and efficiency in the management of the prisons. Two Union officers were the exception to high turnover and reflected the value of longer tenure. Brigadier General Albin F. Schoepf commanded the prison camp at Fort Delaware from April 1863 until January 1866. He improved cleanliness, medical care, and overall prisoner conditions during his time as commander. On June 1, 1864, he issued Special Order 157 detailing cleanliness standards and responsibilities of guards to stop prisoners from slovenly behavior. This order was not taken lightly by guards or prisoners. Schoepf's command resulted in a mortality rate of approximately 11 percent, one of the lowest in all Union camps.[14] Veteran Reserve Corps Colonel (later Brevet Brigadier General) Benjamin J. Sweet commanded Camp Douglas from May 1864 until July 1865. While the death rate was high at the camp, Colonel Sweet's attention to camp and prisoner cleanliness was believed to have saved many prisoner lives. While a strict disciplinarian, Colonel Sweet was respected by the prison population as being fair and consistent.[15]

Another positive example of competent senior commanders in the Union's prison camp system is Lieutenant Colonel William Pierson, first commander at Johnson's Island. Colonel Pierson was the mayor of Sandusky, Ohio, prior to his assignment. His organization, camp structure, and written instructions became a standard for operating procedures that could readily be implemented by camp officers. This organization offered consistent treatment of prisoners in Union prisons for the remainder of the war.

CONCLUSION

Both the Union and the Confederacy based command selection principally on immediate conditions; however, each reacted differently to the assignment of prison camp command. The Union used senior officers; the Confederacy chose junior officers. Excessive turnover of Union commanders resulted in mixed communications with Colonel Hoffman, causing improvements and needs of prisoners to often not

be addressed. Due to the limited influence of Confederate junior officers, while needs were sometimes identified, requests went unan-
swered. Therefore, for different reasons, both Union and
Confederate prisoner of war systems suffered negative impact.

Neither side provided any training for commanders. Both failed
to understand the relationship of commanders to prisoners. Union
and Confederate prison senior commanders demonstrated recogni-
tion of the shortcomings of their command structure yet failed to
take corrective action. Only the Union, eventually with the use of the
Veteran Reserve Corps officers, began to implement solutions to
prison management problems.

With fewer prisons with larger prison population, the Union could
provide senior officers as commanders. On the other hand, the Confederacy's large number of smaller prisons with less prison population led them to select junior officers as commanders.

Clearly, senior officers were superior as camp commanders. The
Confederates either failed to recognize this or refused to free senior
officers from combat duty to manage prisons. The Union recognized
this effect, but by refusing to reduce turnover, mitigated the success
of the senior status. Both sides knew the value of command assign-
ments but took no measures to implement change.

The lack of competent command directly affected the quality of
guards. Selection and training of these guards created additional
poor conditions in prisons.

CHAPTER 7

FACTOR FOUR:
PRISON GUARD SELECTION
AND LACK OF TRAINING

emands for combat soldiers by both sides forced a low priority on selection, equipping, and training of prison guards. Union commander of Camp Douglas Colonel Benjamin Sweet reported to Colonel Hoffman in June 1864 that "These guns [arming stockade guards] have all been condemned, and the inspection and report condemning them forwarded properly, with requests on the part of the commanding officer to the Ordnance Office for new arms and blank requisitions on which to draw them. This was done in February last, since yet nothing has been heard from them."[1]

Guards were the front line of contact with prisoners. The tone set by the guards could establish basic standards for prisoner behavior. Consistent treatment of prisoners by guards was of critical importance in ensuring compliance with prison rules and regulations, but without training for the guards, this was often not the operating procedure.

Author William Hasseltine observed that "In both the North and South the guards were poorly disciplined Home Guards, unfit for more arduous or more responsible service. Captives came into immediate contact with poor personnel and formed their opinions about their captors from the specimens they observed patrolling the prison fences."[2]

Guard forces in both the Union and Confederacy usually consisted of two groups, perimeter guards and "camp police."

Perimeter guards usually patrolled stockade fences, entry points, and stockade guard stations. These guards' primary responsibility was to prevent fence breeches and other escape attempts. They enforced the so-named "deadline," a boundary located a short distance from the stockade fence. Prisoners crossing the line were subject to being shot to death. Armed with rifled muskets or pistols, many of the guards were not even competent enough to fire their weapons. These guards had the least direct contact with prisoners and were often the target of bribery by prisoners for potential escapes.

The camp police were located within the prison compound. They conducted inspections and enforced camp rules. These guards, having the greatest direct contact with prisoners, could make life either miserable or endurable for the prisoners. Examples of brutality and intimidation were most often attributed to these base police groups.

Indiscriminate firing of weapons at prisoners was mentioned often by those incarcerated. Union soldier Henry Eby, 7th Illinois Cavalry, a prisoner at Libby Prison, commented on one use of a weapon by guards: "One day while I was standing near a window, two of my comrades stepped upon the window sill and pulled the window slightly down, to admit some fresh air; when immediately a shot was fired by the guard outside. The ball passed through the window at an angle of about thirty degrees, fortunately missed the boys who opened the window, but passed up through the floor above us, which also contained a large number of prisoners, and unfortunately the ball passed through one of them, severely wounding him."[3]

CONFEDERATE RESPONSE TO PRISON GUARD NEEDS AND TRAINING

Very young or very old aptly describes most Confederate guards. With the large number of smaller prisons, guards were often provided from local sources. Most guard units were either local volunteers or militia. In any case, they were untrained and often poorly armed. In some cases, soldiers unfit for combat were pressed into service. In the Confederacy these compromised soldiers were not as well organized as the Union Veteran Reserve Corps. Nonetheless, they offered some continuity to Confederate prison management. While there was some evidence of brutality, most Confederate guards appeared to conduct their duties with little interest in harassing prisoners. In many instances, the guards' conditions were barely better than the prisoners they were guarding.

Early in the war, Major J. T. W. Harrison, commander of Confederate State Prisons, 1861-1862, in Richmond, reported, "The guard was relieved every morning at nine o'clock, a new regiment being furnished every day at that hour. This regiment was always composed of new recruits, who were sent thither mainly to learn the duties of a soldier. These new recruits were generally so awkward and ineffective that I hazard little in saying there was seldom a day while I was in charge of the rebel prison, when the whole crowd of Federal prisoners-save those who were sick abed in the hospital—might not have marched out and away with impunity."[4]

Union major George Putnam, while a prisoner at Danville, described his Confederate guards, saying: "Our guards represented rather a curious mixture of good-natured indifference and a kind of half-witted cruelty. The officers were, as stated, disabled veterans and were on the whole not a bad lot. This was true also of certain of the sergeants. The rank and file, however, can best be described as scrapings from the mountains. They were mostly slight, overgrown youngsters with less than the proper proportion of wits. They seemed something like the beans that had been given to us in our soup at Libby, not fit for service in the Confederate ranks but good enough for the Yankee prisoners."[5]

As the war continued, there was little change in the poor selection and training of Confederate guards. For example, at Andersonville in mid-1864, Charles H. Thiot, First Georgia Regiment, wrote his wife about some of the reserves. They had, he said, "no more sense than to shoot them [prisoners] if they do cross the line just to pick up a ball or empty a washpan." Thiot later wrote, "some of them would like nothing better than to shoot one of the scoundrels just for the fun of it. Indeed I heard one of them chaps say that he just wanted one to put his foot over the line when he was on post, and he would never give him time to pull it back. Many would murder them in cold blood."[6]

As with problems with prison officers, guard problems were known to prison senior command and were ignored. The need to meet the shortage of men for combat duty appeared more important than prison guarding.

Early in the war, when units were mustering in while prisoners were present, individual organizing units were tasked with providing prison guards. These guards would often be a mixture of new, untrained soldiers from several units.[7] In the last half of 1863, guards at Camp Morton were the recently paroled 51st and 73rd Indiana whose officers were in prison in Richmond. They also lacked noncommissioned officers and were badly demoralized and undisciplined.[8] As the war wore on, a variety of units were assigned as guards. Many were local state volunteer units and militia or units that had earlier been paroled to camps holding prisoners. For example, the Union's 9th Vermont Infantry was paroled to Camp Douglas after the surrender of Harpers Ferry in 1862, and after the exchange they remained, much to their displeasure, at the camp as guards.

There were various examples of nonprofessional military behavior. For example, the guards at Fort Delaware received occasional leave to the Delaware or New Jersey shores. Often guards were intoxicated upon their return to the fort. The access to alcohol off the fort provided easy access to alcohol for soldiers remaining at the fort and also for prisoners. The drinking led to fights among themselves and mistreatment of prisoners.[9]

In mid-1863 the Union's Invalid Corps was organized. This group plus the US Colored Troops became the nucleus of guard forces in the Union. In July of 1864, 350 members of the 16th Veterans Reserve Corps were the first guards at Elmira, New York. [10] The US Colored Troops, while effective, were not well received by Confederate prisoners. Prisoner Walter D. Addison at Point Lookout wrote: "During my entire confinement at Point Lookout were under guard of Negro soldiers whose conduct and treatment of the prisoners was infamously cruel and in many instances, they conducted themselves in a savage manner." According to some, the Negro soldiers treated prisoners with respect. However, most of the prisoners said the Negro guards were seeking revenge against their former masters.[11] While Addison's observation may be true, much of the criticism of Negro guards was a result of racial bias.

Brigadier General Joseph Copeland, commander at the Union's Alton Prison, in May 1864 reported that his guards, the newly recruited Thirteenth Illinois Cavalry, "were imperfectly armed, un-

"Guarding the prisoners. Petersburg, June 30, 1864," sketch by Edwin Forbes. (*Library of Congress*)

drilled, and undisciplined."[12] Colonel Benjamin Sweet at Camp Douglas was concerned when he found that guards from the hundred-day volunteers of the 196th Pennsylvania Infantry had removed the percussion caps from their rifles when they went off shifts, contrary to orders. Further, guard units from the 8th and 15th Veteran Reserve Corps never loaded their weapons.[13]

Rock Island Prison in September 1864 had six different regiments represented in the guard force. Two were hundred-day units and one was known as "The Greybeards."[14]

The Invalid Corps provided a degree of continuity to the Union's organization of guards. As combat veterans they had empathy not found in untrained troops. In 1863, at Rock Island, the Union's Fourth Regiment of the Invalid Corps was reported on by prisoner J. W. Minnich, who said "as a rule they were decent in the treatment of us. I have no complaints to lay against them."[15] Similar comments were made by prisoners at Fort Delaware and Camp Chase.[16] On the other hand, because the corps remained as guards for longer periods of time, any individual intent on brutality was amplified.

Action, such as using the Veteran Reserve Corps and US Colored Troops, addressed concerns of Union camp commanders; however, prison guards continued to have a low priority for the Union.

CONCLUSION

Both North and South prioritized providing guards secondarily, deploying troops to satisfy combat needs. As a result, guards were inexperienced and untrained in the early part of the war.

Both sides identified problems with guards but failed to take significant positive steps to improve the situation. There was no attempt by either side to develop a cadre of professionally trained guards. Implementing the use of Veteran Reserve Corps and US Colored Troops by the North was a positive step. Unfortunately, poor officer leadership reduced the effectiveness of this decision. While wounded and Invalid Corps soldiers were experienced and trained in the military arts, they were untrained in handling prisoners of war. The result was uneven guard support. The Confederacy did little to address the known shortcomings of prison guards. Neither side considered the impact of the guards on discipline, nor on compliance with camp rules and regulations. Military needs of the army were used to justify this inaction.

Assigning those available for duty was the method of selection of guards throughout the war by both the Union and Confederates. Neither the North nor the South appreciated the impact of guards on prisoners and prison life. Attention to this detail could have contributed significantly to the quality of prison camp life.

Coupled with the lack of training of the guards is the fifth factor that significantly affected prison conditions in both North and South: failure to provide individual soldiers with information on how to behave as a prisoner.

CHAPTER 8

FACTOR FIVE:
FAILURE TO PROVIDE SOLDIERS
WITH INFORMATION ON HOW
TO BEHAVE AS PRISONERS

I t is understandable that training of Civil War era soldiers was silent about expectations of a soldier's behavior as a prisoner. The lack of any meaningful history of holding captured combatants as prisoners made such training moot. Additionally, the nineteenth-century military mind thought only in terms of maneuver and weaponry. Teach the soldier how to move and shoot and nothing else was the prevailing philosophy.

Officers were expected to behave with greater military bearing than enlisted men, which contributed to their welfare. Mutual respect and respect for rank and the chain of command was also expected. Generally, officer prisoners received better care from their captors and were in better physical condition than enlisted men. The relatively low Confederate officer death rates at the Union prison for Confederate officers at Johnson's Island and for Union officers in Confederate hands attests to the value of these traits. Union prisoner Lieutenant Cooper indicated a variety of positive activities among prisons at Macon: "In this prison every trade was represented and nearly all were plied to some extent, sometimes for the purpose of gaining a living and sometimes to keep the mind occupied, and to make their quarters more comfortable."[1]

Union colonel Homer Sprague reproduced in his journal the following rules adopted at Danville (Virginia). These rules were typical of expected behavior of Union officers.

RULES UNANIMOUSLY ADOPTED IN THE LOWER ROOM, DANVILLE, VA., PRISON, OCT. 26, 1864:

1. The room shall be thoroughly policed (swept, etc.) four times each day by the messes in succession; viz., at sunrise and sunset, and immediately after breakfast and dinner.

2. There shall be no washing in this room.

3. No emptying slops into spittoons.

4. No washing in the soup buckets or water buckets.

5. No shaking of clothes or blankets in this room.

6. No cooking inside the stoves.

7. No loitering in the yard to the inconvenience of others.

8. No person shall be evidently filthy or infested with vermin.

9. No indecent, profane, or ungentlemanly language in this room.

10. No conduct unbecoming an officer and gentleman about these premises.

11. No talking aloud at night after nine o'clock.

12. An officer of the day shall be appointed daily by the senior officer, whose duty shall be to see that these rules are strictly enforced, and report to the senior officer any violation thereof.

13. In case of any alleged violation of any of these rules, the senior officer of the room shall appoint a Court to consist of thirteen disinterested officers, who shall fairly try and determine the matter, and in case of conviction the offender's rations shall be stopped, or the commander of the prison be requested to confine the offender in a cell according to the sentence of the Court; and it shall be the duty of every officer to have such offender court-martialed after rejoining his command.

For the Committee. H. B. Sprague, Oct. 26, 1864.[2]

CONFEDERATE RESPONSE TO FAILURE TO PROVIDE SOLDIERS WITH INFORMATION ON HOW TO BEHAVE AS PRISONERS

While the Confederacy made no effort to indoctrinate their soldiers on proper behavior, Confederate soldiers of Morgan's Raiders at Camp Chase and Camp Douglas demonstrated actions that would later be included in the US Code of Conduct.

Morgan's Raiders were captured by the Union army in mid-1863. Most were incarcerated in Camp Douglas and Camp Chase. Prior to arrival at Camp Douglas, some of Morgan's Raiders were held at Camp Morton. At Camp Morton they made trouble with a near riot against a group of Tennessee prisoners who had agreed to take the Union's oath of allegiance.[3]

Shortly after Morgan's Raiders' capture, the suspension of the exchange of prisoners was announced. This meant that leaving a prison camp would be by death, escape, signing the Union's oath of allegiance, or the end of the war. Death and the oath of allegiance were not acceptable alternatives to Morgan's Raiders, and the war seemed to be without end. Therefore, escape was the only alternative. Constant attempts to escape, harassing guards, and failing to cooperate with guards were the actions of Morgan's men. Throughout their stay at Camp Douglas and Camp Chase, they were a thorn in the side of their captors.

Morgan's Raiders also protected their fellow troopers. The men would share rations rather than allow a soldier to starve. They attempted to make life as normal as possible. They had a band and a minstrel show, and, at Camp Douglas, they published a newspaper, the *Vidette*, which offered news, political opinion, and classified ads. For example, Abraham Lappin, a prisoner entrepreneur whose business was at Camp Douglas, placed an advertisement in the *Vidette* for handmade smoking pipes, sold, "wholesale and retail at Lappin's factory. Block 17 three doors west of the south east corner. Give him a call you will not be otherwise than satisfied."[4]

Morgan's men were younger, probably more fit than the average population, and were captured in the summer. Nevertheless, they endured two northern winters. Coming from border states, many of them were able to receive packages from home that might include food, clothing, and money. With the strong support of their comrades, Morgan's Raiders had a lower death rate than the general population. A study of Morgan's Raiders at Camp Douglas indicated a death rate of 5 to 7 percent, compared to 15 percent for the general population.[5] The actions of Morgan's Raiders became incorporated into the US Military Code of Conduct enacted in 1955, "resist by any means, make every effort to escape, accept neither parole nor special favors, keep faith in my fellow prisoners."

There were few examples of the type of mutual support shown by Morgan's Raiders in other Union prisons holding Confederate prisoners.

UNION RESPONSE TO FAILURE TO PROVIDE SOLDIERS WITH INFORMATION ON HOW TO BEHAVE AS PRISONERS

As with Confederates, Union leadership saw no reason to address the issue of teaching expected prisoner behavior. Many Union prisoners behaved in an acceptable manner; however, "raiders" at Andersonville and earlier at Belle Isle set the standard for inappropriate behavior as prisoners of war.[6]

Open only fourteen months, Andersonville's 12,919 deaths far exceeded deaths in any other Civil War prison in total number and had nearly the highest death rate among all prisons. The lack of any form of housing, nearly absent medical care, and a hodgepodge of physical organization made Andersonville unmanageable.

Union prisoner Solon Hyde in mid-1864 observed the following of Andersonville prisoners: "It was no uncommon thing to see men wandering in idiocy,—reason, sense, feeling, all dead. This was the saddest of all sights to me. It seemed as though their souls had already taken their departure, leaving the clay tenements to gradual decay. Others again, in apparently as good condition as any of us, and rational in general conversation, could not remember their regiments or the command to which they belonged, while still others could not remember their own names or where they came from."[7]

Andersonville's lack of camp management and prisoner leadership led to the emergence of the "raiders." These criminals, Union soldiers whose genesis was as prisoners at Belle Isle, viciously preyed on their fellow Union captives. Murder, robbery, intimidation, and forcing men to give up their quarters, clothing, bedding, and rations were routine to these depraved individuals. Their actions were ignored by Confederate authorities until a small group of Union prisoners petitioned camp commander Captain Henry Wirz to take action in June 1864.

While the exact number of raiders is unknown, it is estimated that as many as a hundred men participated; Confederate authorities arrested fifty who were tried by a delegation of Union prisoners. Six of the raiders were convicted of murder and sentenced to death by hanging. Others were convicted of lessor crimes with sentences ranging from wearing ball and chain to signs depicting offenses. Prisoners Charles Curtis, Patrick Delaney, John Sarsfield, Cary Sullivan, William Collins, and A. Munn were hanged by Union prisoners at Andersonville on July 10, 1864.

At Union Camp Morton, Confederate prisoners stealing food from others were reported. Food theft was so prevalent that cooks often needed to stand guard, and many prisoners ate their food immediately upon issue.[8]

Other camps, such as Elmira, reported similar behavior. At Elmira, inmate Miles Sherrill reported, "there was a great deal of speculation and swindling carried on in the prison; and I am ashamed to say it, yet it is true that sometimes some of our men were engaged in conspiracy to cheat and defraud their fellow-prisoners."[9]

Tent cutters at Point Lookout roamed the camp, stealing from unattended tents. Prisoner and Confederate soldier Bartlett Y. Mal wrote, "There were some men in camp who had been going about and cutting [tents] and slipping men's hats, boots, and sometimes would get some money. They cut into ours and got money, cloathen amounting to $100. One nite the Negros on gard caught them. They were placed under guard and made to wear a barrel shirt [and marched] up and down the street with the large letters on them. The letters read the 'Tent Cutters'"[10]

Even Union officers were not protected from marauding bands of criminals in Confederate prisons. At Salisbury in 1864, Colonel Homer Sprague wrote in his journal:

> We field officers were quartered that night in a brick building near the entrance, where we passed an hour of horrors. We were attacked by what appeared to be an organized gang of desperadoes, made up of thieves, robbers, Yankee deserters, rebel deserters, and villains generally, maddened by hunger, or bent on plunder, who rejoiced in the euphonious appellation of Muggers! We had been warned against them by kindly disposed guards, and were not wholly unprepared. They attacked us with clubs, fists, and knives, but were repeatedly driven off, pitched headlong downstairs. "Muggers."[11]

There was only scant evidence of Union prisoners, except officers, providing mutual support or respect for their chain of command.

CONCLUSION

As the Confederate prisoners of Morgan's Raiders set the standard for appropriate behavior as prisoners, the "raiders" from the Union army at Andersonville demonstrated the worst in human behavior.

Generally, both Union and Confederate officers reacted more positively to the prison experience than did enlisted men. Military experience with the chain of command and respecting rank likely contributed to this behavior that resulted in reduced mortality.

Neither government can be faulted for not providing training on prisoner behavior early in the war. Had such training been provided when the likelihood of long-term incarceration became evident, it is unknown if it would have resulted in fewer prison deaths. However, based on the information on Morgan's Raiders and Andersonville, it is likely that this training would have been valuable. There was enough down time to provide information to soldiers. Failure to recognize the value of this training likely caused a significant number of deaths in both the North and South prisons.

Regardless, this type of training would have been meaningful during the Civil War. Interestingly, the US military was unable to codify required behavior until 1955.

CHAPTER 9

SUMMARY OF INVESTIGATION RESULTS

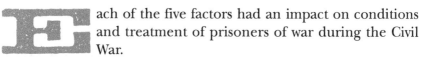ach of the five factors had an impact on conditions and treatment of prisoners of war during the Civil War.

Based on historic treatment of captured combatants, failure to have a strategic plan for administering prisoners before the war was understandable. Shortly before the war, tactical changes resulting in greater mobility and technical innovations of rail and river transportation and the telegraph made it feasible to move and hold prisoners away from combat, rather than using immediate parole and exchange. However, neither army reacted quickly to the impact of these changes as they affected prisoners.

While Union general Meigs recognized the need to handle prisoners, a comprehensive plan for the Union was not developed. Confederate general Winder's approach to prisoners was to react to crises, not to anticipate needs. The lack of strategy resulted in the early inadequate treatment of prisoners on both sides and made inadequate planning the accepted norm, even after the incarceration of large numbers of prisoners became obvious. This initial ignorance of the modern reality of warfare and its impact on captured combatants would haunt the Union and Confederacy throughout the war.

The Union organization for managing prisoners was superior to that of the Confederacy. However, the personal bias and objectives of General Meigs and Colonel Hoffman mitigated this advantage. Both put financial considerations ahead of prisoner welfare. When they realized the need to change their approach, it was too late. Their remedial action was insufficient. Throughout the war, the Union was saddled with prison facilities severely in need of the most basic physical improvements and where care of prisoners was inadequate, especially in terms of nutrition and medical attention.

General Winder lacked resources and organization to manage the prison system. The initial decision to use a large number of small jail and prison facilities and the Confederacy's shortage of experienced officers forced the selection of junior officers, who proved to be ineffective as prison commanders. The result was a decentralized prison system that was nearly impossible to manage.

Even after it became evident that prisoners would be held in camps rather than immediately paroled, neither government developed a plan for long-term incarceration. The immediate needs of the unanticipated large number of prisoners took priority over planning. Both governments were forced to react to immediate problems. General Meigs and Colonel Hoffman continued to act as though parole and exchange would reduce prisoner time in camps. The Union continually deferred identified camp improvements and provided minimal facilities for prisoners. Once long-term incarceration was a reality that could no longer be denied, retrofitting of prisons was hopelessly delinquent. The Union was fortunate in that they selected existing military facilities as the nucleus of the prison system. This system, at least, provided basic housing and reasonably well-developed support facilities.

General Winder and the Confederate government ignored long-term incarceration and reacted to the immediate need to find adequate prison space. Little effort was made to improve the quality of prison life. The early decision to use inadequate, unsupported facilities made matters worse. When hard facilities, such as jails and abandoned buildings, were unavailable, the South was forced to use barren stockades as prisons. These inadequate, unsanitary facilities made basic hygiene and medical care for prisoners impossible. The South either ignored the problem of prisoner care or refused to address the problems. Immediate military needs were often used to justify inactivity and lack of planning by the South.

Neither government took action to improve facilities even when prison populations were low. In mid-1862 and mid-1863, nearly all prisoners, except those too ill to be moved, were exchanged. This was an excellent opportunity to improve existing facilities and to construct additional prison capacity. Instead, the Union assigned junior officers to act as caretakers of facilities that badly needed repairs, and the South improved nothing. This myopic view resulted in inhumane treatment of future prisoners on both sides that could have been anticipated and significantly reduced.

While failing to react to the first two factors has some reasonable rationale, factor three, poor selection and training of commanders, was within the control of both the Union and Confederate governments. The Union selection of senior officers as commanders could have resulted in effective management of the prison system. However, providing no training and allowing excessive command turnover minimized the advantage of rank. The shortcomings of this approach were well understood by senior officers who chose to take little action.

Even if the selection of commanders could not be improved, training of assigned officers should have been implemented. Case after case of poor management and inaccurate record keeping could have been avoided with proper training. There are a few examples of effective camp commanders whose actions had a positive impact on prisons and prisoner care. It is likely that, had more officers with these qualities been assigned as commanders, prison deaths could have been reduced.

The selection of junior officers by the Confederacy guaranteed second-class status to prisons. With limited influence, these junior officers could do little to provide for prisoners. For unknown reasons, other than the press of the war, little was done to guide camp commanders and to provide minimum services to prisoners. There was no evidence of any training for these commanders. General Winder, who was untrained and stretched thin with little staff and significant additional duties, was never able to effectively manage the prison population across the Confederacy.

Both the Union and the Confederacy failed to respond positively to command shortcomings. The problems were known to senior command, and the solutions were within their control. The lack of action caused consistently poor treatment of prisoners. The more effective Union officer structure allowed the North to provide slightly better conditions for prisoners.

Part of the problem for camp commanders was incomplete written directions on their responsibilities. The Dix–Hill Cartel provided no information on handling prisoners other than parole and exchange. General Order 100, published in 1863, provided some guidance to Union commanders. However, General Order 100 contained little to provide camp commanders with information on how to operate a prison. Rather, there were some provisions on treating prisoners and little else of significance to the camp commander. Confederate guidance contained in "Rules and Regulation of the C.S. Military Prisons," published in 1863, provided basic rules for camps with little guidance to commanders on how to operate a prison or treat prisoners.

Neither of these documents were sufficient guidance for camp commanders. Guidance and direction tended to be decentralized in reaction to identified problems or camp command requests. Little was provided broadly to camp commanders. Camp command responsibilities were an afterthought to senior command, leaving implementation to individual, untrained camp commanders.

Like the selection of commanding officers, for both the Union and the Confederacy, the selection and training of guards appeared to be based solely on the immediate availability of personnel. Poorly equipped, trained, and armed guards did very little to support the basic needs of prisoners and, worse, created a dangerous situation for prisoners. Poor discipline and brutality resulted from this lack of training and command indifference. As the first line of contact to prisoners, adequate selection and training of guards could have been effective in improving conditions in both Union and Confederate prisons. Both governments had the authority, power, and understanding to address the selection of these guards. Both sides chose to take no meaningful action.

By mid-1863, the Union effectively employed the Veteran Reserve Corps and US Colored Troops as guards. This change provided better continuity within the prison system. However, because of a lack of guard training and poor command leadership, this structure also provided ample opportunity for brutal guards to terrorize prisoners. In any case, guards continued to be poorly armed and inadequately trained.

The Confederacy continued to use local troops to meet their needs. Beginning in late 1863 and into early 1864, the need to move prisoners ahead of Union military advances placed additional pressure on local guards. Confederate prison facilities opened and closed rapidly, leaving guard requirements in chaos. Often, guards at the new facility were the guards who accompanied prisoners from their former prison. Continued use of very young and very old untrained and ill-equipped guards became the standard in the South. Justification for lack of attention to this detail was given as military necessity.

Both the North and South knew the inefficiency of the guard forces and failed to take meaningful action. The move to noncombat guards by the Union was the only attempt to address the problem. Continued lack of training and command indifference reduced the effectiveness of this move. Confederates were unable or unwilling to correct guard deficiencies.

Not providing training to individual soldiers on expected behavior as a prisoner before the war was understandable. In addition, hidebound military training philosophy did not allow any ancillary training not directly related to fire and maneuver. The Civil War was characterized by large and small engagements followed by periods of rest and refitting. These lulls in battle offered an opportunity to indoctrinate soldiers in behavior expectations, if captured. There is no indication of this being addressed, even though the need for such training was likely known to military leadership.

As prison life became a reality, there was no attempt by either government to provide even minimal information on appropriate prisoner behavior. It appears that neither side wanted to acknowledge the potential capture of their troops. Example after example of violation of the chain of command, failing to assist other prisoners, and acting solely for individual self-interest was evident during the war. The positive effect shown by the actions of Morgan's Raiders and officer prisoners is ample evidence of how effective such training could have been to prisoner survival. Failure to provide this information to soldiers contributed to high death rates in all prisons.

Both the Union and Confederacy failed in their responsibility to provide humane treatment for prisoners. The magnitude of prisoners to be managed overwhelmed both sides. Health risks to all soldiers in the war were magnified in inadequately planned and managed prison camps. The Confederacy merely reacted to needs as they arose. Often their response was to move prisoners to equally poor facilities.

The excuse that the South lacked resources to provide for prisoners is hollow. They were able to equip and feed their army for the term of the war. The Union unquestionably had the resources to provide for prisoners but failed to make adequate food, clothing, and bedding available to prisoners. In Union prisons, a musical chair approach to prison management did nothing for the prisoners. While conditions in Union prisons were superior to those in Confederate facilities, it is difficult to justify the refusal by Colonel Hoffman or camp commanders to provide vegetables for prisoners to reduce diseases such as scurvy. The reduction in rations for prisoners in response to the emaciated condition of Union prisoners released from Belle Isle in May 1864 was a political statement at the expense of proper treatment of individuals.

It is inappropriate to place excessive blame on any single military officer or civilian administrator for many of the deficiencies noted here. The history of captured combatants leading up to the Civil War gave both sides a false expectation of a process for dealing with prisoners. Understanding the changes in technology could have given leadership an indication that the practice of parole would inevitably be replaced by incarceration to handle prisoners of war. Circumstances before and during the war resulted in decisions and actions that, in retrospect, were incorrect or ineffective. It is, however, important that we look at the factors considered here as a measure of what could have been.

Attempting to read the minds of decision makers of the Civil War in the prisoner of war arena during the period is impossible. Perhaps it was simply overwork, ignorance, neglect, or indifference that drove decisions. Or perhaps Carl von Clausewitz was correct in 1832 when he said that prisoners were trophies of war, not humans.

CHAPTER 10

PRISON CAMP SUMMARY: UNION

his chapter contains brief summaries of prison camps discussed throughout this material. The information is intended to be used as a reference for the reader and is not comprehensive.

ALTON PRISON, ILLINOIS
Operated from February 1862 to July 1865.
Prisoners: Enlisted/Political/Irregular forces.
Lack of a strategic plan for prison development and management before and in the early stages of the Civil War:
   Alton was a civilian prison from 1833 until 1860. It remained closed until 1862 when it was opened to relieve crowding at other prisons.
Inadequate plan for long-term incarceration of prisoners of war:
   Existing prison, consisting of three penitentiary buildings, provided basic facilities to house prisoners in conditions similar to civilian prisoners. No water in facilities. Hospital was inadequate and built late.
Poor selection and lack of training of camp command:

There was a high turnover of marginal officers; two commanders were relieved for incompetence. At least six officers served as commanders of the camp. Colonel Weer, who took command in January 1864, was considered a very poor commander and totally incompetent.

Lack of training of camp guards:

Guards were local and represented units of the various commanders. There was a high turnover of guard units. Guards had little or no training.

Failure to provide soldiers information on how to act as POWs:

Camp was overcrowded from its opening in February 1862. High illness and numerous escapes.

CAMP BUTLER, ILLINOIS

Operated from February 1862 to May 1863.

Prisoners: Enlisted.

Lack of a strategic plan for prison development and management before and in the early stages of the Civil War:

Camp Butler was created as a reception center for Union soldiers and converted to a prison camp in February 1862. Necessary improvements to the camp and changes to accommodate prisoners were expensive. Poor sanitation and the effects of weather on the camp were known at the time of opening. Located in the state capital, the camp was unpopular with the population and governor. The camp was totally unprepared to receive the first prisoners from Ft. Donelson, Tennessee.

Inadequate plan for long-term incarceration of prisoners of war:

Frame buildings with no stockade fence until May 1862. Usually overcrowded with tents added. Sanitation and building repairs always needed. Governor warned that strong Southern sympathizers would cause problems.

Poor selection and lack of training of camp command:

Initial commander, Colonel Morrison (February 1862–June 1862) was elderly with marginal performance. He was replaced by Major Fonda (May 1862–January 1863) who improved discipline. Colonel Lynch (January 1863–May 1863) did little to improve facilities and was only concerned about keeping prisoners. There were a total of nine commanders between 1861 and 1865, two during the prisoner exchange in 1862 and one when few prisoners were present in 1863. High turnover was a major factor in conditions at the camp.

Lack of training of camp guards:
Guards came from local units for short periods of time. They received little training; some had no weapons. Prisoner escapes and bribery of guards was common. In 1863, when the 58th Illinois, a combat-experienced unit, became guards, the guarding of prisoners improved.

Failure to provide soldiers information on how to act as POWs:
Health generally poor with many escapes early before the fence was installed.

CAMP CHASE, OHIO

Prisoners from April 1862 to July 1865.

Prisoners: Enlisted/Officers.

Lack of a strategic plan for prison development and management before and in the early stages of the Civil War.
Camp Chase was originally developed as a reception center for Union soldiers and converted to a prison in April 1862. The prison was originally three camps that were consolidated in 1863.

Inadequate plan for long-term incarceration of prisoners of war:
The camp was ill prepared for prisoners from the beginning.

Poor selection and lack of training of camp command:
Commanders were selected because they were available. Turnover was high, with the longest tenure being eight months, until February 1864 when the commander remained in charge until the camp closed. The Ohio governor complained of poor administration.

Lack of training of camp guards:
Escapes, shootings, and general poor training of the Veteran Reserve Corps were evident. Drinking and poor morale of guards were also documented.

Failure to provide soldiers information on how to act as POWs:
Prisoners organized themselves in 1864 to support escapes. Officers and enlisted men, mostly from Morgan's Raiders, were better organized, including a musical band and other recreational activities. Some books and newspapers were available for prisoners. In 1864 a large number of prisoners took the oath of allegiance.

FORT DELAWARE, MARYLAND

Prisoners from May 1862 to June 1865.

Prisoners: Enlisted/Officers/Political.

Lack of a strategic plan for prison development and management before and in the early stages of the Civil War:

> Fort Delaware was an existing fort that was doubled as a prison beginning in May 1862. The fort was used as a staging area for prisoners with many being sent to other prisons or paroled for exchange.

Inadequate plan for long-term incarceration of prisoners of war:

> The fort was extremely wet. Poor-quality barracks were constructed in 1862, but were not sufficient by June 1863. Lack of fresh water was a problem from the beginning. Rain barrels used to collect water were inadequate. The barracks were consistently overcrowded.

Poor selection and lack of training of camp command:

> Until June 1863, four different officers commanded prisoners. Continuity was achieved in June 1863 when Brigadier General Schoepf became commander and remained until June 1865. Schoepf was considered even-handed and effective.

Lack of training of camp guards:

> Most guards were from batteries assigned to the fort and had received no training for their prison duties. The hundred-day unit's (157th Ohio) only service was at Fort Delaware. Desertion, cruelty, and drunkenness were high. There were many reports of guards stealing goods from prisoners that were sent from home

Failure to provide soldiers information on how to act as POWs:

> Officers had special privileges and lived very well. There was a variety of work, such as washers, and opportunities to work outside the fort. There was some cooperation among prisoners to pool money and hire cooks, as well as assist in escapes.

CAMP DOUGLAS, ILLINOIS

Prisoners from February 1862 to July 1865.

Prisoners: Enlisted.

Lack of a strategic plan for prison development and management before and in the early stages of the Civil War:

> Camp Douglas was created as a reception center for Union soldiers and converted to a prison camp in February 1862. Necessary improvements to the camp and changes to accommodate prisoners

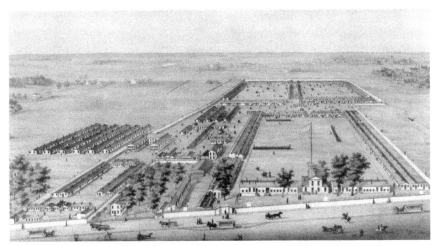

Bird's-eye-view of Camp Douglas, Illinois, in 1864. (*Library of Congress*)

were expensive. Poor sanitation and the effects of weather on the camp were known at the time of opening. Had a strategic plan existed, it is likely that Camp Douglas would not have been selected as a prison; a facility located elsewhere in the Chicago area could have been more secure, been cheaper to build, and offered better sanitation and protection from inclement weather.

Inadequate plan for long-term incarceration of prisoners of war:
The idea that prisoners would be held only briefly resulted in deferral of improvements at Camp Douglas, including building construction and maintenance, sewer construction, and water distribution improvements. When the exchange of prisoners was suspended in mid-1863 the Union realized that prisoners would be held for an extended period. Any attempts to improve conditions came too late, representing a failed attempt to play catch-up.

Poor selection and lack of training of camp command:
Until 1863 when the Invalid Corps (Veteran Reserve Corp) began guarding Camp Douglas, commanders and guards were selected from units mustering in or other untrained commanders. As a result of the lack of strategic plan, officers had no training in the duties of a prison commander and there was no military specialty for managing prisons. Most commanders were eager to take their troops to the war and failed to treat the job as handoff prison com-

mander with any since of urgency. Turnover of command was excessive at Camp Douglas. There were twelve changes of command with nine officers during the camp's existence. In addition, there were three junior officers assigned as commanders when the camp had few, if any, prisoners. This high turnover did not allow for any continuity. New commanders were required to learn fresh the needs of the camp and the prisoners. The lack of pressure on US Army leaders allowed for deferral of projects throughout the life of the camp.

Lack of training of camp guards:

In the early months, camp guards were often conscripted from mustering in units. These soldiers had little, if any, military training. As units were assigned to guard duty, the lack of training as guards was evident. Guards' weapons were old and, on at least one occasion, were condemned and not replaced for over six months. In mid-1863, as Invalid Corps (Veteran Reserve Corp) began guard duty, guard discipline improved; however, training was not increased. Shortage of available guards resulted in assigning a hundred-day unit that was totally unfit to act as guards. While the Invalid Corps (Veteran Reserve Corp) troops were a general improvement, the corps did provide safe haven for brutal guards who found pleasure in mistreating prisoners.

Failure to provide soldiers information on how to act as POWs:

At no time during the Civil War were soldiers trained or indoctrinated in their role as prisoners. The lack of respect for the chain of command, willingness to cooperate with guard authority, mistreatment of fellow prisoners, and total self-protection were typical of captured soldiers. This resulted in the creation of "have" and "have-not" prisoners. Those prisoners with contacts outside the prison, jobs in the prison, friends from former regiments, or other means of support (legal or not) were in the "have" category. Individuals without outside contacts or from isolated units were "have nots." At Camp Douglas, some two thousand Morgan's Raiders were an exception to this general description. These men supported each other, worked to maintain high morale, and protected members of the unit. It is estimated that the mortality of Morgan's Raiders was between 5 and 7 percent, compared to approximately 15 percent for the general population.

ELMIRA, NEW YORK

Prisoners from July 1864 to July 1865.

Prisoners: Enlisted.

Lack of a strategic plan for prison development and management before and in the early stages of the Civil War:

Elmira was created as a reception center for Union soldiers with a separate portion of the facility converted to a prison camp in February 1864 to reduce overcrowding in other camps.

Inadequate plan for long-term incarceration of prisoners of war:

After the suspension of prisoner exchange, one-third of prisoners at Elmira were in tents. Barracks to replace tents were approved in October 1864, and in the winter of that year a third prison in Elmira opened. Barracks were completed in January 1865 for all prisoners, but they were overcrowded. Fosters Pond caused major problems, and the US Army approval was delayed. and corrections made late. Problems with food quality were a result of a complex system of acquisition. Standing water and ineffective sewage removal was a constant problem. Poor medical care contributed to the highest mortality rate of all Union prisons.

Poor selection and lack of training of camp command:

Command had high turnover with no more than four months in command until the fall of 1864 when Colonel Benjamin Tracy remained until the end of the war. Officers of the guard were known to be cruel. Command failed to provide adequate medical treatment.

Lack of training of camp guards:

Even though 350 guards were Veteran Reserve Corps supplemented by 3,000 New York troops, problems existed with quarters for guards resulting in poor performance. Drunkenness, desertion, and cruel treatment of prisoners were noted.

Failure to provide soldiers information on how to act as POWs:

Skating, dancing, and art were common. The camp was divided into groups that lived well and others who had very difficult conditions.

JOHNSON'S ISLAND, OHIO

Prisoners from April 1862 to September 1865.

Prisoners: Officers.

Lack of a strategic plan for prison development and management before and in the early stages of the Civil War:

Johnson's Island was the only prison camp designed and planned by the US Army.

Inadequate plan for long-term incarceration of prisoners of war:
Colonel William Hoffman in 1861 developed the camp as a show-place for a new prison. Well-organized, with books, food, church services, Hoffman underestimated the need for barracks. Poor drainage, limited water, and inclement weather were major problems with the camp.

Poor selection and lack of training of camp command:
Lieutenant Colonel William Pierson was commander from March 1862 to January 1864. He provided detailed written regulations on the operation of the camp. Two commanders subsequent to Pierson were able to manage the camp using these regulations.

Lack of training of camp guards:
Local Ohio units who were trained under the personal supervision of Colonel Hoffman provided most guards through 1864 and represented general good treatment of prisoners. After 1864, guard turnover was high; bribery was common.

Failure to provide soldiers information on how to act as POWs:
Officers were well treated and cooperated well with each other. There was low mortality due, in part, to their positive behavior. Prisoners cooperated in escape attempts.

CAMP MORTON, INDIANA

Prisoners from February 1862 to May 1865.

Prisoners: Enlisted.

Lack of a strategic plan for prison development and management before and in the early stages of the Civil War:
Camp Morton was created as a reception center for Union soldiers and converted to a prison camp in February 1862. Necessary improvements to the camp and changes to accommodate prisoners were expensive and slow in developing.

Inadequate plan for long-term incarceration of prisoners of war:
Conversion and renovation were not done in a timely manner. General conditions, including sanitation and drainage, were poor. Very poor medical care was noted.

Poor selection and lack of training of camp command:
Camp command had high turnover. Except for Colonel David Rose, who served as commander from May 1862 until June 1863,

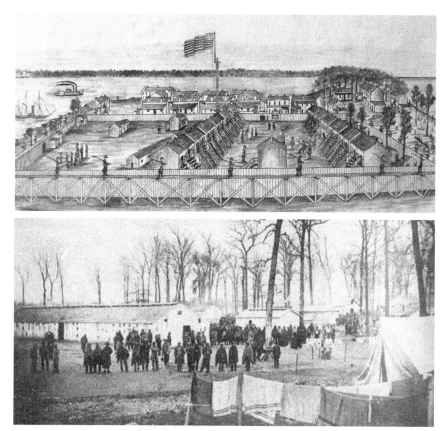

Top, Johnson's Island, Ohio. Bottom, Camp Morton, Indiana. (National Archives)

commanders served for short periods of time. One to three months service was common, with junior officers serving when prison population was low. Colonel Ambrose A. Stevens commanded the camp from October 1863 until the end of the war. He and his command were the Fifth Regiment, Veteran Reserve Corps. There were reports of few attempts by commanders to improve facilities and conditions.

Lack of training of camp guards:

Volunteer guards were mostly Veteran Reserve Corps and were often demoralized. In the spring of 1863, guards were exchanged. Union troops without officers resulted in sadistic treatment of prisoners.

Failure to provide soldiers information on how to act as POWs:
  Prisoners organized a self-government which functioned fairly
  well. Morgan's Raiders prisoners were known to cooperate with
  each other and during escape attempts

POINT LOOKOUT, MARYLAND
Prisoners from June 1863 to July 1865.
Prisoners: Enlisted.
Lack of a strategic plan for prison development and management before and in the early stages of the Civil War:
  The prison camp was located on a low sandy area that held a major
  hospital until the prison camp was added in mid-1863. Although
  there was no planning for stand-alone prisons in the eastern the-
  ater, the camp's location adjacent to a major Union hospital may
  have contributed to the low mortality rate.
Inadequate plan for long-term incarceration of prisoners of war:
  Point Lookout was the first prison opened after the suspension of
  prisoner exchange in 1863 and soon became the largest Union
  prison camp. Secretary Stanton refused to build permanent barracks. Sibley tents were used from the time the camp was opened.
  No reason other than costs was given for the lack of barracks.
Poor selection and lack of training of camp command:
  Brigadier General Gilman Marston opened the camp and commanded from June 1863 to December 1863. From that point, over
  a half-dozen officers commanded the camp for no more than four
  months each. Since few improvements were offered to the camp
  anyway, the lack of continuity was not a major factor in the condi-
  tions in the camp.
Lack of training of camp guards:
  Until February 1864, a variety of untrained volunteer units provided camp guards. From February 1864 until the camp closed,
  US Colored Troops were the primary guards. The soldiers were
  untrained and created significant ill will among the prisoners.
  Shootings by guards and mistreatment were common. This was a
  significant factor in camp conditions.
Failure to provide soldiers information on how to act as POWs:
  Similar to other camps, there was no significant prisoner organization and most prisoners acted as individuals, not part of a military force. Poor cleanliness, depression, gambling, and robbery

Bird's-eye-view of Point Lookout, Maryland, in 1864. (*Library of Congress*)

from fellow prisoners by "tent cutting" were common. Those with special privileges, such as cooks and craftsmen, were singled out by other prisoners.

ROCK ISLAND, ILLINOIS
Prisoners from December 1863 to July 1865.
Prisoners: Enlisted.
Lack of a strategic plan for prison development and management before and in the early stages of the Civil War:
    The location had been a US Army facility since 1804; however, it was inactive prior to the prison camp being established. It was selected as a prison camp and received its first prisoners in December 1863 to relieve crowding in other camps.
Inadequate plan for long-term incarceration of prisoners of war:
    Originally planned as a prison in July 1863, the second prison at Rock Island opened after the suspension of prisoner exchange. Eighty-four 22′ x 10′ barracks were constructed using cheap methods. The prison camp was located on an area of the facility most subject to weather and poor drainage. By the end of the war, the shabbily constructed barracks were in very poor condition and were immediately torn down to make way for the expansion of the arsenal.
Poor selection and lack of training of camp command:
    Colonel A. J. Johnson, experienced at Camp Chase, was com-

mander from January 1864 to July 1865 and represented low turnover of command. Johnson was in conflict with Arsenal Commander major Charles Kingsbury much of the time and was constantly challenged by the *Rock Island Argus*, a Democratic newspaper. The prison population of the camp experienced a fairly low death rate.

Lack of training of camp guards:

Veteran Reserve Corps guards, from November 1863, were reported not properly trained. Hundred-day units guarded prisoners from May 1864. Excessive drinking and shooting of prisoners were noted. Weapons firing by guards going off duty was common. Units guarding included US Colored Troops. The Iowa and Illinois Grey Beards, who were trained to guard railways, were very ineffective.

Failure to provide soldiers information on how to act as POWs:

Some support for escapes. Three hundred of six thousand to ten thousand Confederates who joined the US Navy were from Rock Island. Work details of prisoners were common.

CAMP RANDALL, WISCONSIN

Prisoners from April 1862 to June 1863.

Prisoners: Enlisted.

Lack of a strategic plan for prison development and management before and in the early stages of the Civil War:

The camp, organized to assist in overcrowding, was poorly planned and not prepared to handle prisoners. Medical support was provided from Camp Douglas.

Inadequate plan for long-term incarceration of prisoners of war:

The camp was closed early and not reopened; prisoners transferred to Camp Douglas.

Poor selection and lack of training of camp command:

The camp was open for too short of a time to consider.

Lack of training of camp guards:

The camp was open for too short of a time to consider.

Failure to provide soldiers information on how to act as POWs:

The camp was open for too short of a time to consider.

CHAPTER 11

PRISON CAMP SUMMARY: CONFEDERATE

his chapter contains brief summaries of prison camps discussed throughout this material. The information is intended to be used as a reference for the reader and is not comprehensive.

ANDERSONVILLE, GEORGIA (CAMP SUMTER)
Prisoners from March 1864 to May 1865.
Prisoners: Enlisted.
Lack of a strategic plan for prison development and management before and in the early stages of the Civil War:
>Organized late in the war, Andersonville was a direct result of the lack of a strategic plan.
Inadequate plan for long-term incarceration of prisoners of war:
>This was the only camp "planned" by the Confederacy in 1863; however, the lack of a plan for prisoner care resulted in this facility being poorly located with inadequate local food supply. No clothing or shelter was provided. The only source of water, a stream, was polluted by latrines and the cook house. Medical care was very poor.

Poor selection and lack of training of camp command:
>   Andersonville Commander captain Wirz was the only Confederate officer executed for war crimes as a result of his command at Andersonville.

Lack of training of camp guards:
>   Initially regular troops were used as guards. Reserves consisting of old men and boys, some disabled, were untrained and not respected by prisoners.

Failure to provide soldiers information on how to act as POWs:
>   Some prisoners supported others by digging wells and sharing water. There was no prisoner organization or rules. The camp had a chaotic layout, making organization impossible. Raiders, the nucleus from Belle Isle, were tried and five were hanged. Many prisoners were considered "traitors" and "turncoats."

BELLE ISLE, RICHMOND, VIRGINIA

Prisoners from June 1862 to October 1864.

Prisoners: Enlisted.

Lack of a strategic plan for prison development and management before and in the early stages of the Civil War:
>   Camp was pressed into service when local facilities were fully occupied. This is an excellent example of the result of no strategic plan. Closed September 1862 as prisoners were moved from Richmond, to be reopened in 1863.

Inadequate plan for long-term incarceration of prisoners of war:
>   The camp was considered a temporary facility. Poor quality and old tents were provided in 1863. One-half of prisoners were in tents during the winter of 1863. Prisoners had little clothing, high disease, poor food quality, and a high death rate. Wetness, poor drainage, and the lack of medicine were typical of this camp. The camp reopened in January 1863, closed, and then reopened. In Mach 1864, prisoners were moved to Georgia, and in October 1864, prisoners were moved to Danville and Salisbury. When the camp opened there was little planning for handling prisoners.

Poor selection and lack of training of camp command:
>   Captain Montgomery was well liked. In 1863, Lieutenant Bossiuex was not considered competent.

Lack of training of camp guards:
>   Torture was reported. Clothing and blankets intended for prison-

ers were stolen by guards. Dogs were used against prisoners and shooting of prisoners was common.

Failure to provide soldiers information on how to act as POWs:
>   In 1864, there were frequent reports of prisoners stealing others' food. The camp had its own police (regulators). Fellow prisoner raiders stole from comrades.

BLACKSHEAR, GEORGIA

Prisoners from November 1864 to December 1864.

Prisoners: Enlisted/Political/Irregular forces.

Lack of a strategic plan for prison development and management before and in the early stages of the Civil War:
>   The camp was established hastily as the war ended. There is no evidence of any strategic plan.

Inadequate plan for long-term incarceration of prisoners of war:
>   The camp was hastily developed with no plan. Prisoners were transferred to Charleston partly because of Union military pressure.

Poor selection and lack of training of camp command:
>   The camp was not open long enough to have an impact by commander.

Lack of training of camp guards:
>   Guards used dogs to control prisoners.

Failure to provide soldiers information on how to act as POWs:
>   There was little opportunity for prisoners to organize.

CAHABA, ALABAMA

Prisoners from January 1864 to July 1865.

Prisoners: Enlisted/Political/Irregular forces.

Lack of a strategic plan for prison development and management before and in the early stages of the Civil War:
>   The camp was organized late and reflects no strategic plan.

Inadequate plan for long-term incarceration of prisoners of war:
>   It was located in a cotton warehouse and was very poorly organized. Sanitation was poor with an open trench filled with water. There was no heat; prisoners built fires on dirt floors. In May 1864, prisoners were moved to Andersonville. Prison population increased again through October 1864 with very poor conditions.

Poor selection and lack of training of camp command:
>   Captain Henderson had little or no experience.

Lack of training of camp guards:
  Guards were assigned from untrained local troops.
Failure to provide soldiers information on how to act as POWs:
  There was a mutiny of prisoners in January 1865.

CAMP FORD, TEXAS
Prisoners from July 1863 to July 1865.
Prisoners: Officer/Enlisted.
Lack of a strategic plan for prison development and management before and in the early stages of the Civil War:
  The camp was developed in the second year of the war and was
  not a part of any plan. All but sixty-five prisoners were exchanged
  in December 1863.
Inadequate plan for long-term incarceration of prisoners of war:
  Camp organization reflected no plan for holding prisoners. The
  camp replaced Camp Groce, which was unhealthy and closed after
  one year. A prisoner stockade was added after several months. Initially there were shade trees, but all were eventually cut down for
  shebangs as prisoners built their own shelters. Prisoners increased
  in the spring of 1864, resulting in overcrowding. Scorpions and
  snakes were problems.
Poor selection and lack of training of camp command:
  Captain Warner, Major Tucker, Colonel Allen, Colonel Anderson,
  Lieutenant Colonel Border, and Colonel Sweet reflected the high
  turnover of command.
Lack of training of camp guards:
  Local troops used dogs to control prisoners.
Failure to provide soldiers information on how to act as POWs:
  Prisoners cultivated their own garden (1864). Prisoners published
  their own newspaper. Prisoners built their own shelter (February
  1864). Musical instruments were used to cover escape. Dancing,
  tools, and furniture making existed. Officers were well-organized.

CASTLE THUNDER, RICHMOND, VIRGINIA
Prisoners from August 1862 to April 1865.
Prisoners: Enlisted/Confederate.
Lack of a strategic plan for prison development and management be-
fore and in the early stages of the Civil War:
  The site was used early in the war after local jails and prisons were

full. The prison consisted of three buildings with gaslights and poor ventilation. Reaction to needs was not part of a plan.

Inadequate plan for long-term incarceration of prisoners of war:
In 1862, this camp was planned to be used only as a temporary holding facility. It was closed and reopened in the spring of 1863. Disease (smallpox) was common and ill treatment of prisoners was noted. Facilities were in poor repair with most windows broken. Lack of organization and lack of repairs reflected the lack of planning for long-term incarceration.

Poor selection and lack of training of camp command:
Junior officers were commanding early. Guards were taken by one commander when he was reassigned. In 1863, a senior officer, Lt. Col. Henry Davis, commanded.

Lack of training of camp guards:
Guards used dogs, took money from prisoners, and were known for beatings and theft.

Failure to provide soldiers information on how to act as POWs:
There was no evidence of prisoner organization.

CHARLESTON, SOUTH CAROLINA: SIX LOCATIONS
(Including Castle Pinckney, Liggon's Prison, and Charleston City Jail)
Prisoners from September 1861 to April 1865.
Prisoners: Officers/Enlisted.
Lack of a strategic plan for prison development and management before and in the early stages of the Civil War.
Castle Pinckney was an existing fort abandoned in 1832 and used early in the war. The facility was not crowded at first and was converted to a defensive fortification in 1862. The Charleston City Jail also housed Union prisoners combined with criminals in overcrowded conditions. The facilities were pressed into service without a strategic plan.

Inadequate plan for long-term incarceration of prisoners of war:
Prisons reported poor rations but also reported that rations were better than most. Limited drinking water was a problem. Subject to be fired on by US guns. The prison(s) were not organized for long-term use.

Poor selection and lack of training of camp command:
Junior officers commanded. Nothing done about poor clothing. The Confederate army would not permit replacement of equipment.

Lieutenant F. Millward's sketch of Charleston City Jail was published in the February 18, 1865, edition of *Harper's Weekly*. (*Library of Congress*)

Lack of training of camp guards:

Guards used dogs to control prisoners. Guards were known to fraternize with prisoners.

Failure to provide soldiers information on how to act as POWs:

There was indication of prisoner organization.

COLUMBIA, SOUTH CAROLINA — FOUR LOCATIONS

Prisoners from August 1864 to January 1865.

Prisoners: Officers.

Lack of a strategic plan for prison development and management before and in the early stages of the Civil War:

Prisoners were transferred from Savannah as war pressures required. These locations were not any part of early camp planning. The camp was built in reaction to the increase in prisoners held.

Inadequate plan for long-term incarceration of prisoners of war:

The camp was reported to have poor food quality, although prisoners could buy food. There was no stockade or other shelter provided to prisoners. The only source of water was from a brook.

Poor selection and lack of training of camp command:

Junior officers were in command until Lieutenant Colonel Means, an invalid, become commander in 1864.

Lack of training of camp guards:
> Guards were known to accept bribes. Young cadets were used as guards.

Failure to provide soldiers information on how to act as POWs:
> Prisoners could build their own quarters.

DANVILLE PRISON, VIRGINIA—SIX BUILDINGS, WITH TWO ADDED

Prisoners from November 1863 to April 1865.

Prisoners: Officers/Enlisted, including former enslaved, initially.

Lack of a strategic plan for prison development and management before and in the early stages of the Civil War:
> Not a part of any prewar plan, the prison was developed after suspension of prisoner exchange in 1863. The first prisoners arrived in November 1863.

Inadequate plan for long-term incarceration of prisoners of war:
> There was no plan for long-term incarceration. The facility was crowded with prisoners with inadequate clothing and blankets. The locals wanted the camp closed in 1864.

Poor selection and lack of training of camp command:
> Captain Turner, Major Morfit (October 1864), and Lieutenant Colonel Smith (December 1864) reflected high turnover.

Lack of training of camp guards:
> Corrupt guards traded blankets for food. Guards were reported in poor condition (1864). Guards were unqualified and young. Frequent shootings by guards were reported.

Failure to provide soldiers information on how to act as POWs:
> Many maintained order and discipline. In 1864 a list of rules (dos and don'ts, including cleanliness and order) was created by prisoners.

FLORENCE STOCKADE, SOUTH CAROLINA

Prisoners from September 1864 to February 1865.

Prisoners: Officers/Enlisted, including former enslaved, initially.

Lack of a strategic plan for prison development and management before and in the early stages of the Civil War:
> The camp was opened late in the war for Andersonville prisoners.

Inadequate plan for long-term incarceration of prisoners of war:
> The site was a barren stockade of twenty-three acres with a stockade fence and ditch beyond. No facilities were provided for pris-

oners. The location became extremely overcrowded, with more than 18,000 held and 2,802 deaths, most caused by conditions at Andersonville.

Poor selection and lack of training of camp command:

Colonel George Harrison and Lieutenant Colonel John Iverson (December 1864), 5th Georgia Infantry, were commanders. Harrison was well-liked and considered competent.

Lack of training of camp guards:

Guards came from the 5th Georgia. Some brutality was reported.

Failure to provide soldiers information on how to act as POWs:

Prisoners made their own shebangs from material in area. Most prisoners were in very poor physical condition.

LIBBY PRISON, RICHMOND, VIRGINIA

Prisoners from March 1862 to March 1864.

Prisoners: Officers/Enlisted/Political.

Lack of a strategic plan for prison development and management before and in the early stages of the Civil War:

The early camp was pressed into service after jails and prisons in Richmond were filled. The camp reflected a reaction to needs rather than a strategic plan. The prison had poor lighting; water and toilet facilities needed to be added.

Inadequate plan for long-term incarceration of prisoners of war:

The prison functioned as a distribution point to other prisons. Prisoners were housed in the top two floors. The middle floors were for cooking, and the bottom floors housed the guards. The first prisoners were from other Richmond prisons. By 1863, prisoners reported broken windows, filthy conditions, poor food, and poor heating. In 1864, the prison reported being overcrowded.

Poor selection and lack of training of camp command:

Guards treated prisoners well; shootings and brutality were rare. Camp commanders refused to allow packages for prisoners.

Lack of training of camp guards:

Guards used dogs against prisoners. Strip searches and money taken from prisoners were common. Drunken guards were frequently reported.

Failure to provide soldiers information on how to act as POWs:

Officers and enlisted men were separated. Some diversions were provided, such as music (Libby Minstrels) and books. Escapes and

Camp Oglethorpe, Macon, Georgia, from "The Southern Prisons of the U.S. Officers," Robert J. Fisher, c. 1865.

escape attempts were frequent. Officers only maintained order and discipline.

CAMP OGLETHORPE, MACON, GEORGIA

Prisoners from: Macon 1862–1865, Oglethorpe May 1864–August 1864.

Prisoners: Officers.

Lack of a strategic plan for prison development and management before and in the early stages of the Civil War:

> Camp Oglethorpe had only tents for shelters. No stockade in 1864 reflects the lack of planning. Civilian visits (ladies) were permitted in the main camp.

Inadequate plan for long-term incarceration of prisoners of war:

> The camp was known for lice and filth. Prisoners were moved to Charleston in July 1864 as a result of Union military pressure.

Poor selection and lack of training of camp command:

> Junior officers commanded.

Lack of training of camp guards:

> Drunkenness was common. Old soldiers (veterans) were fair, while home guards were cruel. Some guards were very young.

Failure to provide soldiers information on how to act as POWs:
Confederate money was available (five-to-one US exchange in 1864) for trade. The camp was policed and cleaned by prisoners. A variety of games were played and gambling was common. Prisoners purchased a library for $500.

MILLEN, GEORGIA
Prisoners from October 1864 to December 1864.
Prisoners: Enlisted/Political/Irregular forces.
Lack of a strategic plan for prison development and management before and in the early stages of the Civil War:
The camp was organized late in the war.
Inadequate plan for long-term incarceration of prisoners of war:
Prison was hastily established as the war ended with constant transfers to and from other prisons. The facility was similar to Andersonville but larger. Little planning was evident for its use. The camp was a reaction to immediate needs.
Poor selection and lack of training of camp command:
Captain Vowles reportedly charged prisoners for their exchange.
Lack of training of camp guards:
Reserve regiments were poorly trained and used dogs to control prisoners.
Failure to provide soldiers information on how to act as POWs:
The camp was open too short a time to develop any prisoner organization.

RICHMOND PRISONS, RICHMOND, VIRGINIA
(Including Barrett's Tobacco Factory, Castle Goodwin, Crew & Pemberton Warehouse, Grant's Factory, Gwathmey's Tobacco Warehouse, Harwood's Tobacco Factory, Henrico County Jail, Howard Factory, Ligon's Military Prison, Mayo Factory, Palmer Factory, Ross Factory, Scott's Factory, Smith's Factory, Taylor Factory, and Whitlock's Warehouse.)
Prisoners from July 1861 to April 1865.
Prisoners: Officers/Enlisted.
Lack of a strategic plan for prison development and management before and in the early stages of the Civil War:
All Virginia sites were in reaction to the initial rapid growth to meet requirements from the First Bull Run (three hundred pris-

oners). The camps quickly became very crowded. There was no strategic plan, just a reaction to needs.

Inadequate plan for long-term incarceration of prisoners of war:
By the end of the war one-quarter of Richmond warehouses and factories were converted to prisons. Toilet facilities included open sewers, buckets, and some outside latrines; all were inadequate and poor. Facilities were clearly not planned for long-term incarceration.

Poor selection and lack of training of camp command:
Captains and lieutenants were in command.

Lack of training of camp guards:
Guards were reported drunken and brutal.

Failure to provide soldiers information on how to act as POWs:
Included mixed officers and enlisted, usually on different floors. There was a separate floor for sergeants.

SALISBURY, NORTH CAROLINA
Prisoners from December 1861 to February 1865.
Prisoners: Enlisted/Political/Confederate forces.
Lack of a strategic plan for prison development and management before and in the early stages of the Civil War:
The location was chosen because it was on a major railroad with good food sources. Water and sanitation were good. However, the camp was a reaction to needs not a strategic plan.

Inadequate plan for long-term incarceration of prisoners of war:
In 1862, after exchange became the focal point of prison management, conditions did not improve. Prison population doubled (ten thousand) by October 1864 with transfers from Richmond. There was a lack of medical care, rations, and water. The death rate was higher than Andersonville; most who died had been transferred from Andersonville. There was no action to support long-term incarceration.

Poor selection and lack of training of camp command:
Colonel Gibbs commanded for a few months until he was replaced by Captain Goodwin who was well-liked. Captain Galloway (1863), Colonel Gilmore (July 1864), and Major Gee (September 1864) reflected high turnover of command.

Lack of training of camp guards:
Local students were guards, with some as young as fourteen. In

1864 seniors were added to youth guards.

Failure to provide soldiers information on how to act as POWs:
Escapes were common, but no specific organization among prisoners was reported.

SAVANNAH, GEORGIA: THREE LOCATIONS

Prisoners from July 1864 to October 1864.

Prisoners: Enlisted/Political/Irregular forces.

Lack of a strategic plan for prison development and management before and in the early stages of the Civil War:
The site was used late in the war.

Inadequate plan for long-term incarceration of prisoners of war:
Most prisoners were transfers from Andersonville. An additional stockade was added in September 1864. The camp was used as a reaction to military pressure by the Union.

Poor selection and lack of training of camp command:
Lieutenant Davis commanded in September 1864. He had been a guard at Andersonville.

Lack of training of camp guards:
Guards came from reserves and volunteers, including sailors.

Failure to provide soldiers information on how to act as POWs:
There is no evidence of specific organization of prisoners.

APPENDIX I

List of Prisoners Quoted*

Name	Rank	Army	Unit	Prison held
Addison, Walter D.	Unkn.	C	15th Ala. Inf.	Point Lookout
Bagby, Robert	Pvt.	C	1st NW Mo. Cav.	Camp Douglas
Browne, Junius	Reporter	N/A	N. Y. Tribune	Libby, Salisbury
Burke, Curtis	Pvt.	C	14th Ky. Cav.	Camp Douglas
Coburn, J. Osborn	Pvt.	U	6th Mich. Cav.	Belle Isle
Cooper, Alonzo	Lt.	U	12th N.Y. Cav.	Andersonville, Johnson's Island, Danville, Oglethorpe, Camp Sorghum
Copley, John	Pvt.	C	49th Ten. Inf.	Camp Douglas
Corcoran, Michael	Col.	U	69th N. Y. Inf.	Richmond (Liggon)
Davis, Creed T.				City Point
Davidson, H. M.	Sgt.	U	1st Oh. Lt. Art.	Richmond (Smith Prison), Libby, Andersonville, Danville
Dingman, George	Pvt.	U	27th Mich. Inf.	Belle Isle
Dow, Neal	Brig. Gen.	U	13th Maine Inf.	Libby
Dufur, S. M.	Pvt.	U	1st Vt. Cav.	Belle Isle, Florence
Eby, Henry	Pvt.	U	7th Ill. Cav.	Libby, Belle Isle, Danville, Richmond (Pemberton)
Ferguson, Joseph	Lt.	U	1st N. J. Vol.	Libby, Danville, Macon
Fitts, Lake	Pvt.	U	2nd N.H. Vol.	Salisbury, Richmond (Pemberton)
Frarnsworth, Charles	Lt. Col.	U	1st Conn. Cav.	Libby
Glazier, Willard W.	Cpt.	U	N.Y. Vol. Cav.	Libby, Danville, Oglethorpe, Savannah, Charleston, Columbia (Camp Sorghum)
Huff, William D.	Pvt.	C	13th La. Inf.	Camp Douglas
Hyde, Solon	Hos. St.	U	17th Ohio Inf.	Libby, Danville, Andersonville
Kellogg, Robert	Sgt. Maj.	U	16th Conn. Inf.	Andersonville
Lightcap, W. H.	Pvt.	U	5th Ia. Cav.	Andersonville
Lyons, W. F.	Pvt.	U	9th Min. Inf.	Andersonville, Oglethorpe
Malone, Bartlett Y.	Unkn.	C	Unknown	Point Lookout
Minnich, J. W.	Unkn.	C	Unknown	Rock Island
Murray, John O.	Maj.	C		Ft. Delaware, Morris Island
Putnam, George	Maj.	U	176th N.Y. Vol.	Danville
Ransom, John	Pvt.	U	6th Mich. Cav.	Richmond (Liggon)
Roach, A. C.	Lt.	U	51st Ind. Vol.	Libby, Charleston, Columbia

.

Name	Rank	Army	Unit	Prison held
Shepard, Henry	Lt.	C	Unknown	Johnson's Island
Smedley, Charles	Cpl.	U	90th Penn Inf.	Danville, Andersonville, Florence
Sprague, Homer	Col.	U	18th Conn. Vol.	Salisbury, Danville
Urban, John	Unkn.	U	Unknown	Florence
Urban, W. A.	Cpt.	C	1st Penn. Inf.	Johnson's Island
Warren, Leroy	Unkn.	U	Unknown	Richmond (Atkinson)
Wells, James T .	Unkn.	C	Unknown	Point Lookout

*The sources for the quotes are found in the bibliography under each soldier's name, except the following that are quoted from secondary sources and detailed in the notes: Addison, Chap. 7, note 11; Coburn, Chap. 3, note 28; Corcoran, Chap. 3, note 43; Dingman, Chap. 3, note 42; Dow, Chap. 3, note 61; Fitts, Chap. 3, note 83; Farnsworth, Chap. 3, note 36; Malone, Chap. 8, note 10; Minnich, Chap. 7, note 15.

APPENDIX II

Confederate Prison Camps Studied

Prison	Type	Date First Prisoners Arrived	Date First Prisoners Left	Most Prisoners Held*	Official Deaths
Andersonville, GA (Camp Sumter)	Barren stockade	1864	1865	32,899	12,919
Belle Isle, VA	Barren stockade	1862	1864	10,000	300+
Blackshear, GA	Barren stockade	1864	1864	5,000	
Cahaba, AL	Converted building	1863	1865	3,000	225?
Camp Ford, TX	Barren stockade	1863	1865	4,900	232+
Castle Thunder, VA	Converted building	1862	1865	3,000	
Charleston, SC Six locations	Existing prisons and converted buildings; coastal fortification	1861	1865	1,100	
Columbia, SC Four locations	Existing prisons and converted buildings, tents, and open area	1864	1865	2,000	2,000
Danville, VA	Converted building	1863	1865	4,000	1,297
Florence, SC	Barren stockade	1864	1865	1,500	2,820
Libby Warehouse, VA	Converted building	1862	1865	4,221	20+
Macon, GA (Camp Oglethorpe)	Existing prisons and converted buildings, fairgrounds	1861	1864	1,900	
Millen, GA	Barren stockade	1864	1864	10,299	488+
Richmond VA Fifteen locations	Existing prisons, converted buildings	1861	1865	13,500	200+
Salisbury, NC	Converted buildings, tents	1861	1865	10,321	3,700
Savannah, GA Three locations	Existing prisons, tents, open area	1864	1864	6,000	2+?
TOTALS				113,640	22,203

*As a result of transfers near the end of the war there are duplicate counts in these numbers.

APPENDIX III

Union Prison Camps Studied

Prison	Type	Date First Prisoners Arrived	Date First Prisoners Left	Total Prisoners Held (Est.)	Most Prisoners Held At One Time	Official Deaths	Death Rate
Point Lookout, MD	Tents with high fences	July	June	52,000	22,000	3,584	.06
Fort Delaware, DE	Coastal fort	May	June	25,300	12,600	2,416	9
Camp Douglas, IL	Barracks with high fences	Feb	July	30,000	12,082	4,454	15
Elmira, NY	Barracks with high fences	July	July	12,200	9,441	2,933	24
Camp Chase, OH	Barracks with high fences	April	July	16,300	9,423	2,260	13
Rock Island, IL	Barracks with high fences	Dec	July	12,200	8,670	1,960	16
Camp Morton, IN	Converted buildings, high fences	Feb	May	12,100	5,000	1,763	10
Johnson's Island, OH	Barracks with high fences fair ground	April	Sep	7,600	3,256	235	.03
Alton, IL	Existing prison	Feb	June	9,300	1,891	1,508	16
Camp Butler, IL	Barracks with high fences	Feb	May	5,500	2,186	866	16
Camp Randall, WI	Barracks without fences	April	June	1,300	1,300	139	11
TOTALS				183,800	87,849	22,118	

APPENDIX IV

Dix–Hill Cartel

Source: *Official Records of the War of Rebellion* (Washington: US Government Printing Office, 1901) Series II, Volume 4, 266–68

July 22, 1862

The undersigned having been commissioned by the authorities they respectively represent to make arrangements for a general exchange of prisoners of war have agreed to the following articles:

ARTICLE 1. It is hereby agreed and stipulated that all prisoners of war held by either party including those taken on private armed vessels known as privateers shall be discharged upon the conditions and terms following:

Prisoners to be exchanged man for man and officer for officer; privateers to be placed upon the footing of officers and men of the Navy. Men and officers of lower grades may be exchanged for officers of a higher grade, and men and officers of different services may be exchanged according to the following scale of equivalents:

A general commanding in chief or an admiral shall be exchanged for officers of equal rank, or for sixty privates or common seamen.

A flag officer or major general shall be exchanged for officers of equal rank, or for forty privates or common seamen.

A commodore carrying a broad pennant or a brigadier-general shall be exchanged for officers of equal rank, or twenty privates or common seamen.

A captain in the Navy or a colonel shall be exchanged for officers of equal rank, or for fifteen privates or common seamen.

A lieutenant-colonel or a commander in the Navy shall be exchanged for officers of equal rank, or for 10 privates or common seamen.

A lieutenant-commander or a major shall be exchanged for officers of equal rank, or eight privates or common seamen.

A lieutenant or a master in the Navy or a captain in the Army or marines shall be exchanged for officers of equal rank, or six privates or common seamen.

Masters' mates in the Navy or lieutenants and ensigns in the Army or marines shall be exchanged for officers of equal rank, or four privates or common seamen.

Midshipmen, warrant officers in the Navy, masters of merchant vessels and commanders of privateers shall be exchanged for officers of equal rank, or three privates or common seamen.

Second captains, lieutenants or mates of merchant vessels or privateers and all petty officers in the Navy and all non-commissioned officers in the Army or marines shall be severally exchanged for persons of equal rank, or for two privates or common seamen, and private soldiers or common seamen shall be exchanged for each other, man for man.

ARTICLE 2. Local, State, civil and militia rank held by persons not in actual military service will not be recognized, the basis of exchange being the grade actually held in the naval and military service of the respective parties.

ARTICLE 3. If citizens held by either party on charges of disloyalty or any alleged civil offense are exchanged it shall be only for citizens. Captured sutlers, teamsters and all civilians in the actual service of either party to be exchanged for persons in similar position.

ARTICLE 4. All prisoners of war to be discharged on parole in 10 days after their capture, and the prisoners now held and those hereafter taken to be transported to the points mutually agreed upon at the expense of the capturing party. The surplus prisoners not exchanged shall not be permitted to take up arms again, nor to serve as military police or constabulary force in any fort, garrison, or field-work held by either of the respective parties, nor as guards of prisons, depots or stores, nor to discharge any duty usually performed by soldiers, until exchanged under the provisions of this cartel. The exchange is not to be considered complete until the officer or soldier exchanged for has been actually restored to the lines to which he belongs.

ARTICLE 5. Each party upon the discharge of prisoners of the other party is authorized to discharge an equal number of their own officers or men from parole, furnishing at the same time to the other party a list of the prisoners discharged and of their own officers and men relieved from parole, thus enabling each party to relieve from parole such of their own officers and men as the party may choose. The lists thus mutually furnished will keep both parties advised of the true condition of the exchange of prisoners.

ARTICLE 6. The stipulations and provisions above mentioned to be of binding obligation during the continuance of the war, it matters not which party may have the surplus of prisoners, the great principles involved being, first, an equitable exchange of prisoners, man for man, officer for officer, or officers of higher grade exchanged for officers of lower grade or for privates, according to the scale of equivalents; second, that privateers and officers and men of different services may be exchanged according to the same scale of equivalents; third, that all prisoners, of whatever arm of service, are to be exchanged or paroled in 10 days from the time of their capture, if it be practicable to transfer them to their own lines in that time; if not, as soon thereafter as practicable; fourth, that no officer, soldier, or employee, in the service of either party, is to be considered as exchanged and absolved from his parole until his equivalent has actually reached the lines of his friends; fifth, that the parole forbids the performance of field, garrison, police, or guard, or constabulary duty.

JOHN A. DIX Major General, U.S. Army

D. H. HILL Major-General, C.S. Army

SUPPLEMENTARY ARTICLES.

ARTICLE 7. All prisoners of war now held on either side and all prisoners hereafter taken shall be sent with all reasonable dispatch to A. M. Aiken's, below Dutch Gap, on the James River, Va., or to Vicksburg, on the Mississippi River, in the State of Mississippi, and there exchanged or paroled until such exchange can be effected, notice being previously given by each party of the number of prisoners it will send and the time when they will be delivered at those points respectively; and in case the vicissitudes of war shall change the military relations of the places designated in this article to the contending parties so as to render the same inconvenient for the delivery and exchange of prisoners, other places bearing as nearly as may be the present local relations of said places to the lines of said parties shall be by mutual agreement substituted. But nothing in this article contained shall prevent the commanders of two opposing armies from exchanging prisoners or releasing them on parole from other points mutually agreed on by said commanders.

ARTICLE 8. For the purpose of carrying into effect the foregoing articles of agreement each party will appoint two agents, to be called agents for the exchange of prisoners of war, whose duty it shall be to communicate with each other by correspondence and otherwise, to prepare the lists of prisoners, to attend to the delivery of the prisoners at the places agreed on and to carry out promptly, effectually and in good faith all the details and provisions of the said articles of agreement.

ARTICLE 9. And in case any misunderstanding shall arise in regard to any clause or stipulation in the foregoing articles it is mutually agreed that such misunderstanding shall not interrupt the release of prisoners on parole, as herein provided, but shall be made the subject of friendly explanations in order that the object of this agreement may neither be defeated nor postponed.

JOHN A. DIX Major-General, U.S. Army

D. H. HILL Major-General, C.S. Army

APPENDIX V

US General Order 100

Source: *Official Records of the War of Rebellion* (Washington: US Government Printing Office, 1901) Series II, Volume 5, 671–682.

GENERAL ORDER 100
Prepared by Francis Lieber, promulgated as General Order No. 100 by President Lincoln, 24 April 1863.

SECTION I. Martial Law—Military jurisdiction—Military necessity—Retaliation

Article 1. A place, district, or country occupied by an enemy stands, in consequence of the occupation, under the Martial Law of the invading or occupying army, whether any proclamation declaring Martial Law, or any public warning to the inhabitants, has been issued or not. Martial Law is the immediate and direct effect and consequence of occupation or conquest.

The presence of a hostile army proclaims its Martial Law.

Art. 2. Martial Law does not cease during the hostile occupation, except by special proclamation, ordered by the commander in chief; or by special mention in the treaty of peace concluding the war, when the occupation of a place or territory continues beyond the conclusion of peace as one of the conditions of the same.

Art. 3. Martial Law in a hostile country consists in the suspension, by the occupying military authority, of the criminal and civil law, and of the domestic administration and government in the occupied place or territory, and in the substitution of military rule and force for the same, as well as in the dictation of general laws, as far as military necessity requires this suspension, substitution, or dictation.

The commander of the forces may proclaim that the administration of all civil and penal law shall continue either wholly or in part, as in times of peace, unless otherwise ordered by the military authority.

Art. 4. Martial Law is simply military authority exercised in accordance with the laws and usages of war. Military oppression is not Martial Law: it is the abuse of the power which that law confers. As Martial Law is executed by military force, it is incumbent upon those who administer it to be strictly guided by the principles of justice, honor, and humanity—virtues adorning a soldier even more than other men, for the very reason that he possesses the power of his arms against the unarmed.

Art. 5. Martial Law should be less stringent in places and countries fully occupied and fairly conquered. Much greater severity may be exercised in places or regions where actual hostilities exist, or are expected and must be prepared for. Its most complete sway is allowed—even in the commander's own country—when face to face with the enemy, because of the absolute necessities of the case, and of the paramount duty to defend the country against invasion.

To save the country is paramount to all other considerations.

Art. 6. All civil and penal law shall continue to take its usual course in the enemy's places and territories under Martial Law, unless interrupted or stopped by order of the occupying military power; but all the functions of the hostile government—legislative executive, or administrative—whether of a general, provincial, or local character, cease under Martial Law, or continue only with the sanction, or, if deemed necessary, the participation of the occupier or invader.

Art. 7. Martial Law extends to property, and to persons, whether they are subjects of the enemy or aliens to that government.

Art. 8. Consuls, among American and European nations, are not diplomatic agents. Nevertheless, their offices and persons will be subjected to Martial Law in cases of urgent necessity only: their property and business are not exempted. Any delinquency they commit against the established military rule may be punished as in the case of any other inhabitant, and such punishment furnishes no reasonable ground for international complaint.

Art. 9. The functions of Ambassadors, Ministers, or other diplomatic agents accredited by neutral powers to the hostile government, cease, so far as regards the displaced government; but the conquering or occupying power usually recognizes them as temporarily accredited to itself.

Art. 10. Martial Law affects chiefly the police and collection of public revenue and taxes, whether imposed by the expelled government or by the invader, and refers mainly to the support and efficiency of the army, its safety, and the safety of its operations.

Art. 11. The law of war does not only disclaim all cruelty and bad faith concerning engagements concluded with the enemy during the war, but also the breaking of stipulations solemnly contracted by the belligerents in time of peace, and avowedly intended to remain in force in case of war between the contracting powers.

It disclaims all extortions and other transactions for individual gain; all acts of private revenge, or connivance at such acts.

Offenses to the contrary shall be severely punished, and especially so if committed by officers.

Art. 12. Whenever feasible, Martial Law is carried out in cases of individual offenders by Military Courts; but sentences of death shall be executed only with the approval of the chief executive, provided the urgency of the case does not require a speedier execution, and then only with the approval of the chief commander.

Art. 13. Military jurisdiction is of two kinds: First, that which is conferred and defined by statute; second, that which is derived from the common law of war. Military offenses under the statute law must be tried in the manner therein directed; but military offenses which do not come within the statute must be tried and punished under the common law of war. The character of the courts which exercise these jurisdictions depends upon the local laws of each particular country.

In the armies of the United States the first is exercised by courts-martial, while cases which do not come within the "Rules and Articles of War," or the jurisdiction conferred by statute on courts-martial, are tried by military commissions.

Art. 14. Military necessity, as understood by modern civilized nations, consists in the necessity of those measures which are indispensable for securing the ends of the war, and which are lawful according to the modern law and usages of war.

Art. 15. Military necessity admits of all direct destruction of life or limb of armed enemies, and of other persons whose destruction is incidentally unavoidable in the armed contests of the war; it allows of the capturing of every armed enemy, and every enemy of importance to the hostile government, or of peculiar danger to the captor; it allows of all destruction of property, and obstruction of the ways and channels of traffic, travel, or communication, and of all withholding of sustenance or means of life from the enemy; of the appropriation of whatever an enemy's country affords necessary for the subsistence and safety of the army, and of such deception as does not involve the breaking of good faith either positively pledged, regarding agreements entered into during the war, or supposed by the modern law of war to exist. Men who take up arms against one another in public war do not cease on this account to be moral beings, responsible to one another and to God.

Art. 16. Military necessity does not admit of cruelty—that is, the infliction of suffering for the sake of suffering or for revenge, nor of maiming or wounding except in fight, nor of torture to extort confessions. It does not admit of the use of poison in any way, nor of the wanton devastation of a district. It admits of deception, but disclaims acts of perfidy; and, in general, military necessity does not include any act of hostility which makes the return to peace unnecessarily difficult.

Art. 17. War is not carried on by arms alone. It is lawful to starve the hostile belligerent, armed or unarmed, so that it leads to the speedier subjection of the enemy.

Art. 18. When a commander of a besieged place expels the noncombatants, in order to lessen the number of those who consume his stock of provisions, it is lawful, though an extreme measure, to drive them back, so as to hasten on the surrender.

Art. 19. Commanders, whenever admissible, inform the enemy of their intention to bombard a place, so that the noncombatants, and especially the women and children, may be removed before the bombardment commences. But it is no infraction of the common law of war to omit thus to inform the enemy. Surprise may be a necessity.

Art. 20. Public war is a state of armed hostility between sovereign nations or governments. It is a law and requisite of civilized existence that men live in political, continuous societies, forming organized units, called states or nations, whose constituents bear, enjoy, suffer, advance and retrograde together, in peace and in war.

Art. 21. The citizen or native of a hostile country is thus an enemy, as one of the constituents of the hostile state or nation, and as such is subjected to the hardships of the war.

Art. 22. Nevertheless, as civilization has advanced during the last centuries, so has likewise steadily advanced, especially in war on land, the distinction between the private individual belonging to a hostile country and the hostile country itself, with its men in arms. The principle has been more and more acknowledged that the unarmed citizen is to be spared in person, property, and honor as much as the exigencies of war will admit.

Art. 23. Private citizens are no longer murdered, enslaved, or carried off to distant parts, and the inoffensive individual is as little disturbed in his private relations as the commander of the hostile troops can afford to grant in the overruling demands of a vigorous war.

Art. 24. The almost universal rule in remote times was, and continues to be with barbarous armies, that the private individual of the hostile country is destined to suffer every privation of liberty and protection, and every disruption of family ties. Protection was, and still is with uncivilized people, the exception.

Art. 25. In modern regular wars of the Europeans, and their descendants in other portions of the globe, protection of the inoffensive citizen of the hostile country is the rule; privation and disturbance of private relations are the exceptions.

Art. 26. Commanding generals may cause the magistrates and civil officers of the hostile country to take the oath of temporary allegiance or an oath of fidelity to their own victorious government or rulers, and they may expel everyone who declines to do so. But whether they do so or not, the people and their civil officers owe strict obedience to them as long as they hold sway over the district or country, at the peril of their lives.

Art. 27. The law of war can no more wholly dispense with retaliation than can the law of nations, of which it is a branch. Yet civilized nations acknowledge retaliation as the sternest feature of war. A reckless enemy often leaves to his opponent no other means of securing himself against the repetition of barbarous outrage

Art. 28. Retaliation will, therefore, never be resorted to as a measure of mere revenge, but only as a means of protective retribution, and moreover, cautiously and unavoidably; that is to say, retaliation shall only be resorted to after careful inquiry into the real occurrence, and the character of the misdeeds that may demand retribution.

Unjust or inconsiderate retaliation removes the belligerents farther and farther from the mitigating rules of regular war, and by rapid steps leads them nearer to the internecine wars of savages.

Art. 29. Modern times are distinguished from earlier ages by the existence, at one and the same time, of many nations and great governments related to one another in close intercourse.

Peace is their normal condition; war is the exception. The ultimate object of all modern war is a renewed state of peace.

The more vigorously wars are pursued, the better it is for humanity. Sharp wars are brief.

Art. 30. Ever since the formation and coexistence of modern nations, and ever since wars have become great national wars, war has come to be acknowledged not to be its own end, but the means to obtain great ends of state, or to consist in defense against wrong; and no conventional restriction of the modes adopted to injure the enemy is any longer admitted; but the law of war imposes many limitations and restrictions on principles of justice, faith, and honor.

SECTION II. Public and private property of the enemy—Protection of persons, and especially of women, of religion, the arts and sciences—Punishment of crimes against the inhabitants of hostile countries.

Art. 31. A victorious army appropriates all public money, seizes all public movable property until further direction by its government, and sequesters for its own benefit or of that of its government all the revenues of real property belonging to the hostile government or nation. The title to such real property remains in abeyance during military occupation, and until the conquest is made complete.

Art. 32. A victorious army, by the martial power inherent in the same, may suspend, change, or abolish, as far as the martial power extends, the relations which arise from the services due, according to the existing laws of the invaded country, from one citizen, subject, or native of the same to another.

The commander of the army must leave it to the ultimate treaty of peace to settle the permanency of this change.

Art. 33. It is no longer considered lawful—on the contrary, it is held to be a serious breach of the law of war—to force the subjects of the enemy into the service of the victorious government, except the latter should proclaim, after a fair and complete conquest of the hostile country or district, that it is resolved to keep the country, district, or place permanently as its own and make it a portion of its own country.

Art. 34. As a general rule, the property belonging to churches, to hospitals, or other establishments of an exclusively charitable character, to establishments of education, or foundations for the promotion of knowledge, whether public schools, universities, academies of learning or observatories, museums of the fine arts, or of a scientific character such property is not to be considered public property in the sense of paragraph 31; but it may be taxed or used when the public service may require it.

Art. 35. Classical works of art, libraries, scientific collections, or precious instruments, such as astronomical telescopes, as well as hospitals, must be secured against all avoidable injury, even when they are contained in fortified places whilst besieged or bombarded.

Art. 36. If such works of art, libraries, collections, or instruments belonging to a hostile nation or government, can be removed without injury, the ruler of the conquering state or nation may order them to be seized and removed for the benefit of the said nation. The ultimate ownership is to be settled by the ensuing treaty of peace.

In no case shall they be sold or given away, if captured by the armies of the United States, nor shall they ever be privately appropriated, or wantonly destroyed or injured.

Art. 37. The United States acknowledge and protect, in hostile countries occupied by them, religion and morality; strictly private property; the persons of the inhabitants, especially those of women: and the sacredness of domestic relations. Offenses to the contrary shall be rigorously punished.

This rule does not interfere with the right of the victorious invader to tax the people or their property, to levy forced loans, to billet soldiers, or to appropriate property, especially houses, lands, boats or ships, and churches, for temporary and military uses

Art. 38. Private property, unless forfeited by crimes or by offenses of the owner, can be seized only by way of military necessity, for the support or other benefit of the army or of the United States.

If the owner has not fled, the commanding officer will cause receipts to be given, which may serve the spoliated owner to obtain indemnity.

Art. 39. The salaries of civil officers of the hostile government who remain in the invaded territory, and continue the work of their office, and can continue it according to the circumstances arising out of the war—such as judges, administrative or police officers, officers of city or communal governments—are paid from the public revenue of the invaded territory, until the military government has reason wholly or partially to discontinue it. Salaries or incomes connected with purely honorary titles are always stopped.

Art. 40. There exists no law or body of authoritative rules of action between hostile armies, except that branch of the law of nature and nations which is called the law and usages of war on land.

Art. 41. All municipal law of the ground on which the armies stand, or of the countries to which they belong, is silent and of no effect between armies in the field.

Art. 42. Slavery, complicating and confounding the ideas of property, (that is of a thing,) and of personality, (that is of humanity,) exists according to municipal or local law only. The law of nature and nations has never acknowledged it. The digest of the Roman law enacts the early dictum of the pagan jurist, that "so far as the law of nature is concerned, all men are equal." Fugitives escaping from a country in which they were slaves, villains, or serfs, into another country, have, for centuries past, been held free and acknowledged free by judicial decisions of European countries, even though the municipal law of the country in which the slave had taken refuge acknowledged slavery within its own dominions.

Art. 43. Therefore, in a war between the United States and a belligerent which admits of slavery, if a person held in bondage by that belligerent be captured by or come as a fugitive under the protection of the military forces of the United States, such person is immediately entitled to the rights and privileges of a freeman To return such person into slavery would amount to enslaving a free person, and neither the United States nor any officer under their authority can enslave any human being. Moreover, a person so made free by the law of war is under the shield of the law of nations, and the former owner or State can have, by the law of postliminy, no belligerent lien or claim of service.

Art. 44. All wanton violence committed against persons in the invaded country, all destruction of property not commanded by the authorized officer, all robbery, all pillage or sacking, even after taking a place by main force, all rape, wounding, maiming, or killing of such inhabitants, are prohibited under the penalty of death, or such other severe punishment as may seem adequate for the gravity of the offense.

A soldier, officer or private, in the act of committing such violence, and disobeying a superior ordering him to abstain from it, may be lawfully killed on the spot by such superior.

Art. 45. All captures and booty belong, according to the modern law of war, primarily to the government of the captor.

Prize money, whether on sea or land, can now only be claimed under local law.

Art. 46. Neither officers nor soldiers are allowed to make use of their position or power in the hostile country for private gain, not even for commercial transactions otherwise legitimate. Offenses to the contrary committed by commissioned officers will be punished with cashiering or such other punishment as the nature of the offense may require; if by soldiers, they shall be punished according to the nature of the offense.

Art. 47. Crimes punishable by all penal codes, such as arson, murder, maiming, assaults, highway robbery, theft, burglary, fraud, forgery, and rape, if committed by an American soldier in a hostile country against its inhabitants, are not only punishable as at home, but in all cases in which death is not inflicted, the severer punishment shall be preferred.

SECTION III. Deserters—Prisoners of war—Hostages—Booty on the battle-field.

Art. 48. Deserters from the American Army, having entered the service of the enemy, suffer death if they fall again into the hands of the United States, whether by capture, or being delivered up to the American Army; and if a deserter from the enemy, having taken service in the Army of the United States, is captured by the enemy, and punished by them with death or otherwise, it is not a breach against the law and usages of war, requiring redress or retaliation.

Art. 49. A prisoner of war is a public enemy armed or attached to the hostile army for active aid, who has fallen into the hands of the captor, either fighting or wounded, on the field or in the hospital, by individual surrender or by capitulation.

All soldiers, of whatever species of arms; all men who belong to the rising en masse of the hostile country; all those who are attached to the army for its efficiency and promote directly the object of the war, except such as are hereinafter provided for; all disabled men or officers on the field or elsewhere, if captured; all enemies who have thrown away their arms and ask for quarter, are prisoners of war, and as such exposed to the inconveniences as well as entitled to the privileges of a prisoner of war.

Art. 50. Moreover, citizens who accompany an army for whatever purpose, such as sutlers, editors, or reporters of journals, or contractors, if captured, may be made prisoners of war, and be detained as such.

The monarch and members of the hostile reigning family, male or female, the chief, and chief officers of the hostile government, its diplomatic agents, and all persons who are of particular and singular use and benefit to the hostile army or its government, are, if captured on belligerent ground, and if unprovided with a safe conduct granted by the captor's government, prisoners of war.

Art. 51. If the people of that portion of an invaded country which is not yet occupied by the enemy, or of the whole country, at the approach of a hostile army, rise, under a duly authorized levy en masse to resist the invader, they are now treated as public enemies, and, if captured, are prisoners of war.

Art. 52. No belligerent has the right to declare that he will treat every captured man in arms of a levy en masse as a brigand or bandit. If, however, the people of a country, or any portion of the same, already occupied by an army, rise against it, they are violators of the laws of war, and are not entitled to their protection.

Art. 53. The enemy's chaplains, officers of the medical staff, apothecaries, hospital nurses and servants, if they fall into the hands of the American Army, are not prisoners of war, unless the commander has reasons to retain them. In this latter case; or if, at their own desire, they are allowed to remain with their captured companions, they are treated as prisoners of war, and may be exchanged if the commander sees fit.

Art. 54. A hostage is a person accepted as a pledge for the fulfillment of an agreement concluded between belligerents during the war, or in consequence of a war. Hostages are rare in the present age.

Art. 55. If a hostage is accepted, he is treated like a prisoner of war, according to rank and condition, as circumstances may admit.

Art. 56. A prisoner of war is subject to no punishment for being a public enemy, nor is any revenge wreaked upon him by the intentional infliction of any suffering, or disgrace, by cruel imprisonment, want of food, by mutilation, death, or any other barbarity.

Art. 57. So soon as a man is armed by a sovereign government and takes the soldier's oath of fidelity, he is a belligerent; his killing, wounding, or other warlike acts are not individual crimes or offenses. No belligerent has a right to declare that enemies of a certain class, color, or condition, when properly organized as soldiers, will not be treated by him as public enemies.

Art. 58. The law of nations knows of no distinction of color, and if an enemy of the United States should enslave and sell any captured persons of their army, it would be a case for the severest retaliation, if not redressed upon complaint.

The United States cannot retaliate by enslavement; therefore death must be the retaliation for this crime against the law of nations.

Art. 59. A prisoner of war remains answerable for his crimes committed against the captor's army or people, committed before he was captured, and for which he has not been punished by his own authorities.

All prisoners of war are liable to the infliction of retaliatory measures.

Art. 60. It is against the usage of modern war to resolve, in hatred and revenge, to give no quarter. No body of troops has the right to declare that it will not give, and therefore will not expect, quarter; but a commander is permitted to direct his troops to give no quarter, in great straits, when his own salvation makes it impossible to cumber himself with prisoners.

Art. 61. Troops that give no quarter have no right to kill enemies already disabled on the ground, or prisoners captured by other troops.

Art. 62. All troops of the enemy known or discovered to give no quarter in general, or to any portion of the army, receive none.

Art. 63. Troops who fight in the uniform of their enemies, without any plain, striking, and uniform mark of distinction of their own, can expect no quarter.

Art. 64. If American troops capture a train containing uniforms of the enemy, and the commander considers it advisable to distribute them for use among his men, some striking mark or sign must be adopted to distinguish the American soldier from the enemy.

Art. 65. The use of the enemy's national standard, flag, or other emblem of nationality, for the purpose of deceiving the enemy in battle, is an act of perfidy by which they lose all claim to the protection of the laws of war.

Art. 66. Quarter having been given to an enemy by American troops, under a misapprehension of his true character, he may, nevertheless, be ordered to suffer death if, within three days after the battle, it be discovered that he belongs to a corps which gives no quarter.

Art. 67. The law of nations allows every sovereign government to make war upon another sovereign state, and, therefore, admits of no rules or laws different from those of regular warfare, regarding the treatment of prisoners of war, although they may belong to the army of a government which the captor may consider as a wanton and unjust assailant.

Art. 68. Modern wars are not internecine wars, in which the killing of the enemy is the object. The destruction of the enemy in modern war, and, indeed, modern war itself, are means to obtain that object of the belligerent which lies beyond the war.

Unnecessary or revengeful destruction of life is not lawful.

Art. 69. Outposts, sentinels, or pickets are not to be fired upon, except to drive them in, or when a positive order, special or general, has been issued to that effect.

Art. 70. The use of poison in any manner, be it to poison wells, or food, or arms, is wholly excluded from modern warfare. He that uses it puts himself out of the pale of the law and usages of war.

Art.71. Whoever intentionally inflicts additional wounds on an enemy already wholly disabled, or kills such an enemy, or who orders or encourages soldiers to do so, shall suffer death, if duly convicted, whether he belongs to the Army of the United States, or is an enemy captured after having committed his misdeed.

Art. 72. Money and other valuables on the person of a prisoner, such as watches or jewelry, as well as extra clothing, are regarded by the American Army as the private property of the prisoner, and the appropriation of such valuables or money is considered dishonorable, and is prohibited. Nevertheless, if large sums are found upon the persons of prisoners, or in their possession, they shall be taken from them, and the surplus, after providing for their own support, appropriated for the use of the army, under the direction of the commander, unless otherwise ordered by the government. Nor can prisoners claim, as private property, large sums found and captured in their train, although they have been placed in the private luggage of the prisoners.

Art. 73. All officers, when captured, must surrender their side arms to the captor. They may be restored to the prisoner in marked cases, by the commander, to signalize admiration of his distinguished bravery or approbation of his humane treatment of prisoners before his capture. The captured officer to whom they may be restored cannot wear them during captivity.

Art. 74. A prisoner of war, being a public enemy, is the prisoner of the government, and not of the captor. No ransom can be paid by a prisoner of war to his individual captor or to any officer in command. The government alone releases captives, according to rules prescribed by itself.

Art. 75. Prisoners of war are subject to confinement or imprisonment such as may be deemed necessary on account of safety, but they are to be subjected to no other intentional suffering or indignity. The confinement and mode of treating a prisoner may be varied during his captivity according to the demands of safety.

Art. 76. Prisoners of war shall be fed upon plain and wholesome food, whenever practicable, and treated with humanity.

They may be required to work for the benefit of the captor's government, according to their rank and condition.

Art. 77. A prisoner of war who escapes may be shot or otherwise killed in his flight; but neither death nor any other punishment shall be inflicted upon him simply for his attempt to escape, which the law of war does not consider a crime. Stricter means of security shall be used after an unsuccessful attempt at escape.

If, however, a conspiracy is discovered, the purpose of which is a united or general escape, the conspirators may be rigorously punished, even with death; and capital punishment may also be inflicted upon prisoners of war discovered to have plotted rebellion against the authorities of the captors, whether in union with fellow prisoners or other persons.

Art. 78. If prisoners of war, having given no pledge nor made any promise on their honor, forcibly or otherwise escape, and are captured again in battle after having rejoined their own army, they shall not be punished for their escape, but shall be treated as simple prisoners of war, although they will be subjected to stricter confinement.

Art. 79. Every captured wounded enemy shall be medically treated, according to the ability of the medical staff.

Art. 80. Honorable men, when captured, will abstain from giving to the enemy information concerning their own army, and the modern law of war permits no longer the use of any violence against prisoners in order to extort the desired information or to punish them for having given false information.

SECTION IV. Partisans—Armed enemies not belonging to the hostile army—Scouts—Armed prowlers—War-rebels

Art. 81. Partisans are soldiers armed and wearing the uniform of their army, but belonging to a corps which acts detached from the main body for the purpose of making inroads into the territory occupied by the enemy. If captured, they are entitled to all the privileges of the prisoner of war.

Art. 82. Men, or squads of men, who commit hostilities, whether by fighting, or inroads for destruction or plunder, or by raids of any kind, without commission, without being part and portion of the organized hostile army, and without sharing continuously in the war, but who do so with intermitting returns to their homes and avocations, or with the occasional assumption of the semblance of peaceful pursuits, divesting themselves of the character or appearance of soldiers—such men, or squads of men, are not public enemies, and, therefore, if captured, are not entitled to the privileges of prisoners of war, but shall be treated summarily as highway robbers or pirates.

Art. 83. Scouts, or single soldiers, if disguised in the dress of the country or in the uniform of the army hostile to their own, employed in obtaining information, if found within or lurking about the lines of the captor, are treated as spies, and suffer death.

Art. 84. Armed prowlers, by whatever names they may be called, or persons of the enemy's territory, who steal within the lines of the hostile army for the purpose of robbing, killing, or of destroying bridges, roads or canals, or of robbing or destroying the mail, or of cutting the telegraph wires, are not entitled to the privileges of the prisoner of war.

Art. 85. War-rebels are persons within an occupied territory who rise in arms against the occupying or conquering army, or against the authorities established by the same. If captured, they may suffer death, whether they rise singly, in small or large bands, and whether called upon to do so by their own, but expelled, government or not. They are not prisoners of war; nor are they if discovered and secured before their conspiracy has matured to an actual rising or armed violence.

SECTION V. Safe-conduct—Spies—War-traitors—Captured messengers—Abuse of the flag of truce

Art. 86. All intercourse between the territories occupied by belligerent armies, whether by traffic, by letter, by travel, or in any other way, ceases. This is the general rule, to be observed without special proclamation.

Exceptions to this rule, whether by safe-conduct, or permission to trade on a small or large scale, or by exchanging mails, or by travel from one territory into the other, can take place only according to agreement approved by the government, or by the highest military authority.

Contraventions of this rule are highly punishable.

Art. 87. Ambassadors, and all other diplomatic agents of neutral powers, accredited to the enemy, may receive safe-conducts through the territories occupied by the belligerents, unless there are military reasons to the contrary, and unless they may reach the place of their destination conveniently by another route. It implies no international affront if the safe-conduct is declined. Such passes are usually given by the supreme authority of the State, and not by subordinate officers.

Art. 88. A spy is a person who secretly, in disguise or under false pretense, seeks information with the intention of communicating it to the enemy.

The spy is punishable with death by hanging by the neck, whether or not he succeed in obtaining the information or in conveying it to the enemy.

Art. 89. If a citizen of the United States obtains information in a legitimate manner, and betrays it to the enemy, be he a military or civil officer, or a private citizen, he shall suffer death.

Art. 90. A traitor under the law of war, or a war-traitor, is a person in a place or district under Martial Law who, unauthorized by the military commander, gives information of any kind to the enemy, or holds intercourse with him.

Art. 91. The war-traitor is always severely punished. If his offense consists in betraying to the enemy anything concerning the condition, safety, operations, or plans of the troops holding or occupying the place or district, his punishment is death.

Art. 92. If the citizen or subject of a country or place invaded or conquered gives information to his own government, from which he is separated by the hostile army, or to the army of his government, he is a war-traitor, and death is the penalty of his offense.

Art. 93. All armies in the field stand in need of guides, and impress them if they cannot obtain them otherwise.

Art. 94. No person having been forced by the enemy to serve as guide is punishable for having done so.

Art. 95. If a citizen of a hostile and invaded district voluntarily serves as a guide to the enemy, or offers to do so, he is deemed a war-traitor, and shall suffer death.

Art. 96. A citizen serving voluntarily as a guide against his own country commits treason, and will be dealt with according to the law of his country.

Art. 97. Guides, when it is clearly proved that they have misled intentionally, may be put to death.

Art. 98. An unauthorized or secret communication with the enemy is considered treasonable by the law of war.

Foreign residents in an invaded or occupied territory, or foreign visitors in the same, can claim no immunity from this law. They may communicate with foreign parts, or with the inhabitants of the hostile country, so far as the military authority permits, but no further. Instant expulsion from the occupied territory would be the very least punishment for the infraction of this rule.

Art. 99. A messenger carrying written dispatches or verbal messages from one portion of the army, or from a besieged place, to another portion of the same army, or its government, if armed, and in the uniform of his army, and if captured, while doing so, in the territory occupied by the enemy, is treated by the captor as a prisoner of war. If not in uniform, nor a soldier, the circumstances connected with his capture must determine the disposition that shall be made of him.

Art. 100. A messenger or agent who attempts to steal through the territory occupied by the enemy, to further, in any manner, the interests of the enemy, if captured, is not entitled to the privileges of the prisoner of war, and may be dealt with according to the circumstances of the case.

Art. 101. While deception in war is admitted as a just and necessary means of hostility, and is consistent with honorable warfare, the common law of war allows even capital punishment for clandestine or treacherous attempts to injure an enemy, because they are so dangerous, and it is difficult to guard against them.

Art. 102. The law of war, like the criminal law regarding other offenses, makes no difference on account of the difference of sexes, concerning the spy, the war-traitor, or the war-rebel.

Art. 103. Spies, war-traitors, and war-rebels are not exchanged according to the common law of war. The exchange of such persons would require a special cartel, authorized by the government, or, at a great distance from it, by the chief commander of the army in the field.

Art. 104. A successful spy or war-traitor, safely returned to his own army, and afterwards captured as an enemy, is not subject to punishment for his acts as a spy or war-traitor, but he may be held in closer custody as a person individually dangerous.

SECTION VI. Exchange of prisoners—Flags of truce—Flags of protection

Art. 105. Exchanges of prisoners take place—number for number—rank for rank wounded for wounded—with added condition for added condition—such, for instance, as not to serve for a certain period.

Art. 106. In exchanging prisoners of war, such numbers of persons of inferior rank may be substituted as an equivalent for one of superior rank as may be agreed upon by cartel, which requires the sanction of the government, or of the commander of the army in the field.

Art. 107. A prisoner of war is in honor bound truly to state to the captor his rank; and he is not to assume a lower rank than belongs to him, in order to cause a more advantageous exchange, nor a higher rank, for the purpose of obtaining better treatment.

Offenses to the contrary have been justly punished by the commanders of released prisoners, and may be good cause for refusing to release such prisoners.

Art. 108. The surplus number of prisoners of war remaining after an exchange has taken place is sometimes released either for the payment of a stipulated sum of money, or, in urgent cases, of provision, clothing, or other necessaries.

Such arrangement, however, requires the sanction of the highest authority.

Art. 109. The exchange of prisoners of war is an act of convenience to both belligerents. If no general cartel has been concluded, it cannot be demanded by either of them. No belligerent is obliged to exchange prisoners of war.

A cartel is voidable as soon as either party has violated it.

Art. 110. No exchange of prisoners shall be made except after complete capture, and after an accurate account of them, and a list of the captured officers, has been taken.

Art. 111. The bearer of a flag of truce cannot insist upon being admitted. He must always be admitted with great caution. Unnecessary frequency is carefully to be avoided.

Art. 112. If the bearer of a flag of truce offer himself during an engagement, he can be admitted as a very rare exception only. It is no breach of good faith to retain such flag of truce, if admitted during the engagement. Firing is not required to cease on the appearance of a flag of truce in battle.

Art. 113. If the bearer of a flag of truce, presenting himself during an engagement, is killed or wounded, it furnishes no ground of complaint whatever.

Art. 114. If it be discovered, and fairly proved, that a flag of truce has been abused for surreptitiously obtaining military knowledge, the bearer of the flag thus abusing his sacred character is deemed a spy.

So sacred is the character of a flag of truce, and so necessary is its sacredness, that while its abuse is an especially heinous offense, great caution is requisite, on the other hand, in convicting the bearer of a flag of truce as a spy.

Art. 115. It is customary to designate by certain flags (usually yellow) the hospitals in places which are shelled, so that the besieging enemy may avoid firing on them. The same has been done in battles, when hospitals are situated within the field of the engagement.

Art. 116. Honorable belligerents often request that the hospitals within the territory of the enemy may be designated, so that they may be spared. An honorable belligerent allows himself to be guided by flags or signals of protection as much as the contingencies and the necessities of the fight will permit.

Art. 117. It is justly considered an act of bad faith, of infamy or fiendishness, to deceive the enemy by flags of protection. Such act of bad faith may be good cause for refusing to respect such flags.

Art. 118. The besieging belligerent has sometimes requested the besieged to designate the buildings containing collections of works of art, scientific museums, astronomical observatories, or precious libraries, so that their destruction may be avoided as much as possible.

SECTION VII. Parole

Art. 119. Prisoners of war may be released from captivity by exchange, and, under certain circumstances, also by parole.

Art. 120. The term Parole designates the pledge of individual good faith and honor to do, or to omit doing, certain acts after he who gives his parole shall have been dismissed, wholly or partially, from the power of the captor.

Art. 121. The pledge of the parole is always an individual, but not a private act.

Art. 122. The parole applies chiefly to prisoners of war whom the captor allows to return to their country, or to live in greater freedom within the captor's country or territory, on conditions stated in the parole.

Art. 123. Release of prisoners of war by exchange is the general rule; release by parole is the exception.

Art. 124. Breaking the parole is punished with death when the person breaking the parole is captured again.

Accurate lists, therefore, of the paroled persons must be kept by the belligerents.

Art. 125. When paroles are given and received there must be an exchange of two written documents, in which the name and rank of the paroled individuals are accurately and truthfully stated.

Art. 126. Commissioned officers only are allowed to give their parole, and they can give it only with the permission of their superior, as long as a superior in rank is within reach.

Art. 127. No noncommissioned officer or private can give his parole except through an officer. Individual paroles not given through an officer are not only void, but subject the individuals giving them to the punishment of death as deserters. The only admissible exception is where individuals, properly separated from their commands, have suffered long confinement without the possibility of being paroled through an officer.

Art. 128. No paroling on the battlefield; no paroling of entire bodies of troops after a battle; and no dismissal of large numbers of prisoners, with a general declaration that they are paroled, is permitted, or of any value. Art. 129. In capitulations for the surrender of strong places or fortified camps the commanding officer, in cases of urgent necessity, may agree that the troops under his command shall not fight again during the war, unless exchanged.

[There was no article 129 in the original document.]

Art. 130. The usual pledge given in the parole is not to serve during the existing war, unless exchanged.

This pledge refers only to the active service in the field, against the paroling belligerent or his allies actively engaged in the same war. These cases of breaking the parole are patent acts, and can be visited with the punishment of death; but the pledge does not refer to internal service, such as recruiting or drilling the recruits, fortifying places not besieged, quelling civil commotions, fighting against belligerents unconnected with the paroling belligerents, or to civil or diplomatic service for which the paroled officer may be employed.

Art. 131. If the government does not approve of the parole, the paroled officer must return into captivity, and should the enemy refuse to receive him, he is free of his parole.

Art. 132. A belligerent government may declare, by a general order, whether it will allow paroling, and on what conditions it will allow it. Such order is communicated to the enemy.

Art. 133. No prisoner of war can be forced by the hostile government to parole himself, and no government is obliged to parole prisoners of war, or to parole all captured officers, if it paroles any. As the pledging of the parole is an individual act, so is paroling, on the other hand, an act of choice on the part of the belligerent.

Art. 134. The commander of an occupying army may require of the civil officers of the enemy, and of its citizens, any pledge he may consider necessary for the safety or security of his army, and upon their failure to give it he may arrest, confine, or detain them.

SECTION VIII. Armistice—Capitulation

Art. 135. An armistice is the cessation of active hostilities for a period agreed between belligerents. It must be agreed upon in writing, and duly ratified by the highest authorities of the contending parties.

Art. 136. If an armistice be declared, without conditions, it extends no further than to require a total cessation of hostilities along the front of both belligerents.

If conditions be agreed upon, they should be clearly expressed, and must be rigidly adhered to by both parties. If either party violates any express condition, the armistice may be declared null and void by the other.

Art. 137. An armistice may be general, and valid for all points and lines of the belligerents, or special, that is, referring to certain troops or certain localities only.

An armistice may be concluded for a definite time; or for an indefinite time, during which either belligerent may resume hostilities on giving the notice agreed upon to the other.

Art. 138. The motives which induce the one or the other belligerent to conclude an armistice, whether it be expected to be preliminary to a treaty of peace, or to prepare during the armistice for a more vigorous prosecution of the war, does in no way affect the character of the armistice itself.

Art. 139. An armistice is binding upon the belligerents from the day of the agreed commencement; but the officers of the armies are responsible from the day only when they receive official information of its existence.

Art. 140. Commanding officers have the right to conclude armistices binding on the district over which their command extends, but such armistice is subject to the ratification of the superior authority, and ceases so soon as it is made known to the enemy that the armistice is not ratified, even if a certain time for the elapsing between giving notice of cessation and the resumption of hostilities should have been stipulated for.

Art. 141. It is incumbent upon the contracting parties of an armistice to stipulate what intercourse of persons or traffic between the inhabitants of the territories occupied by the hostile armies shall be allowed, if any.

If nothing is stipulated the intercourse remains suspended, as during actual hostilities.

Art. 142. An armistice is not a partial or a temporary peace; it is only the suspension of military operations to the extent agreed upon by the parties.

Art. 143. When an armistice is concluded between a fortified place and the army besieging it, it is agreed by all the authorities on this subject that the besieger must cease all extension, perfection, or advance of his attacking works as much so as from attacks by main force.

But as there is a difference of opinion among martial jurists, whether the besieged have the right to repair breaches or to erect new works of defense within the place during an armistice, this point should be determined by express agreement between the parties.

Art. 144. So soon as a capitulation is signed, the capitulator has no right to demolish, destroy, or injure the works, arms, stores, or ammunition, in his possession, during the time which elapses between the signing and the execution of the capitulation, unless otherwise stipulated in the same.

Art. 145. When an armistice is clearly broken by one of the parties, the other party is released from all obligation to observe it.

Art. 146. Prisoners taken in the act of breaking an armistice must be treated as prisoners of war, the officer alone being responsible who gives the order for such a violation of an armistice. The highest authority of the belligerent aggrieved may demand redress for the infraction of an armistice.

Art. 147. Belligerents sometimes conclude an armistice while their plenipotentiaries are met to discuss the conditions of a treaty of peace; but plenipotentiaries may meet without a preliminary armistice; in the latter case, the war is carried on without any abatement.

SECTION IX. Assassination

Art. 148. The law of war does not allow proclaiming either an individual belonging to the hostile army, or a citizen, or a subject of the hostile government, an outlaw, who may be slain without trial by any captor, any more than the modern law of peace allows such intentional outlawry; on the contrary, it abhors such outrage. The sternest retaliation should follow the murder committed in consequence of such proclamation, made by whatever authority. Civilized nations look with horror upon offers of rewards for the assassination of enemies as relapses into barbarism.

SECTION X. Insurrection—Civil War—Rebellion

Art. 149. Insurrection is the rising of people in arms against their government, or a portion of it, or against one or more of its laws, or against an officer or officers of the government. It may be confined to mere armed resistance, or it may have greater ends in view.

Art. 150. Civil war is war between two or more portions of a country or state, each contending for the mastery of the whole, and each claiming to be the legitimate government. The term is also sometimes applied to war of rebellion, when the rebellious provinces or portions of the state are contiguous to those containing the seat of government.

Art. 151. The term rebellion is applied to an insurrection of large extent, and is usually a war between the legitimate government of a country and portions of provinces of the same who seek to throw off their allegiance to it and set up a government of their own.

Art. 152. When humanity induces the adoption of the rules of regular war to ward rebels, whether the adoption is partial or entire, it does in no way whatever imply a partial or complete acknowledgement of their government, if they have set up one, or of them, as an independent and sovereign power. Neutrals have no right to make the adoption of the rules of war by the assailed government toward rebels the ground of their own acknowledgment of the revolted people as an independent power.

Art. 153. Treating captured rebels as prisoners of war, exchanging them, concluding of cartels, capitulations, or other warlike agreements with them; addressing officers of a rebel army by the rank they may have in the same; accepting flags of truce; or, on the other hand, proclaiming Martial Law in their territory, or levying war-taxes or forced loans, or doing any other act sanctioned or demanded by the law and usages of public war between sovereign belligerents, neither proves nor establishes an acknowledgment of the rebellious people, or of the government which they may have erected, as a public or sovereign power. Nor does the adoption of the rules of war toward rebels imply an engagement with them extending beyond the limits of these rules. It is victory in the field that ends the strife and settles the future relations between the contending parties.

Art. 154. Treating, in the field, the rebellious enemy according to the law and usages of war has never prevented the legitimate government from trying the leaders of the rebellion or chief rebels for high treason, and from treating them accordingly, unless they are included in a general amnesty.

Art. 155. All enemies in regular war are divided into two general classes—that is to say, into combatants and noncombatants, or unarmed citizens of the hostile government.

The military commander of the legitimate government, in a war of rebellion, distinguishes between the loyal citizen in the revolted portion of the country and the disloyal citizen. The disloyal citizens may further be classified into those citizens known to sympathize with the rebellion without positively aiding it, and those who, without taking up arms, give positive aid and comfort to the rebellious enemy without being bodily forced thereto.

Art. 156. Common justice and plain expediency require that the military commander protect the manifestly loyal citizens, in revolted territories, against the hardships of the war as much as the common misfortune of all war admits.

The commander will throw the burden of the war, as much as lies within his power, on the disloyal citizens, of the revolted portion or province, subjecting them to a stricter police than the noncombatant enemies have to suffer in regular war; and if he deems it appropriate, or if his government demands of him that every citizen shall, by an oath of allegiance, or by some other manifest act, declare his fidelity to the legitimate government, he may expel, transfer, imprison, or fine the revolted citizens who refuse to pledge themselves anew as citizens obedient to the law and loyal to the government.

Whether it is expedient to do so, and whether reliance can be placed upon such oaths, the commander or his government have the right to decide.

Art. 157. Armed or unarmed resistance by citizens of the United States against the lawful movements of their troops is levying war against the United States, and is therefore treason.

APPENDIX VI

Rules and Regulation of the CS Military Prisons

Source: http://www.civilwarrichmond.com

1863

All orders affecting prisoners of war and the general discipline of the entire command, will be issued by the officer commanding; an order proceeding from any other source will not be regarded by officers on duty at the prisons.

There will be a roll call daily of prisoners at 7 1/2 A.M., and at 6 P.M., and the officer of the guard must be present at each.

No prisoner, whatever his rank, will be allowed to leave the quarters, to which he is assigned, under any pretext whatever, without special permission from the officer commanding; nor shall any prisoner be fired upon by a sentinel or other person except in case of revolt or attempted escape.

No letters, packages, or parcels of any kind can be passed into the prison or hospital, without first being examined by the officer commanding, or the Surgeon of the post.

Prisoners are not allowed to have any communications with persons outside of the prison, and no visitor will be allowed an interview with a prisoner without the permission from the Brigadier General commanding the Department of Henrico. from Hd. Qrs.

Prisoners are not allowed to converse with sentinels; nor must they congregate about the windows after dark.

The firing of one gun at night, or two during the day, will be the signal for immediate assembling of the guard.

Under no circumstances will sentinels be allowed to sit down upon post, or to rest their guns on the ground.

At 9 o'clock P.M., the lights throughout the prison, except in the hospital and officer's quarters, must be immediately extinguished; and it shall be the duty of the Officer of the Guard to inspect the prison at that hour, to see that the lights are put out, fire secured, and that everything is quiet.

No conversation, intercourse, or trading with the prisoners, in any manner whatever, will be allowed.

The Officer of the Guard must not be absent at any one time from his post for a period exceeding one hour.

The guard off post must remain constantly at the guard house ready for instant service, and their guns must be kept on the rack.

Every guard room must be policed each morning by the old guard and will not be received, by the officer of the new guard unless in good order. Both the officers of the old and new guard will be held responsible for the execution of this order, and also for the safe keeping of all articles left in the guard house.

These rules and regulations must be read to the new guard every morning before posting the first relief.

(signed)

Th. P. Turner, Major Comd'g

Approved John H. Winder, Brig. Gen. Comd'g Dept. Henrico

APPENDIX VII

Graphic Representation of Study Results

The following are results of the importance of the five factors in each prison camp in the initial studies sponsored by the Andersonville National Site POW Research Program. Camps were rated on a score of five (being the most important impact of the five factors on the camp) to one (being the least important). The graph is courtesy of *MI Magazine.*

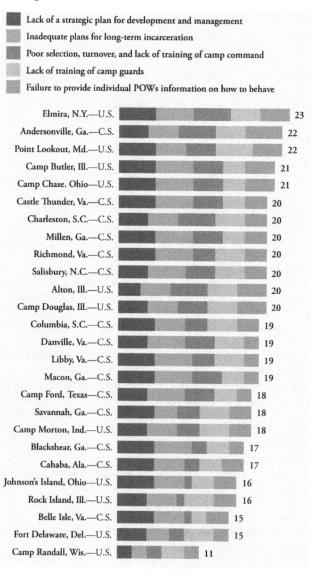

▉	Lack of a strategic plan for development and management
▉	Inadequate plans for long-term incarceration
▉	Poor selection, turnover, and lack of training of camp command
▉	Lack of training of camp guards
▉	Failure to provide individual POWs information on how to behave

Camp	Score
Elmira, N.Y.—U.S.	23
Andersonville, Ga.—C.S.	22
Point Lookout, Md.—U.S.	22
Camp Butler, Ill.—U.S.	21
Camp Chase. Ohio—U.S.	21
Castle Thunder, Va.—C.S.	20
Charleston, S.C.—C.S.	20
Millen, Ga.—C.S.	20
Richmond, Va.—C.S.	20
Salisbury, N.C.—C.S.	20
Alton, Ill.—U.S.	20
Camp Douglas, Ill.—U.S.	20
Columbia, S.C.—C.S.	19
Danville, Va.—C.S.	19
Libby, Va.—C.S.	19
Macon, Ga.—C.S.	19
Camp Ford, Texas—C.S.	18
Savannah, Ga.—C.S.	18
Camp Morton, Ind.—U.S.	18
Blackshear, Ga.—C.S.	17
Cahaba, Ala.—C.S.	17
Johnson's Island, Ohio—U.S.	16
Rock Island, Ill.—U.S.	16
Belle Isle, Va.—C.S.	15
Fort Delaware, Del.—U.S.	15
Camp Randall, Wis.—U.S.	11

NOTES

INTRODUCTION
1. US Sanitary Commission, *Narrative of Privations and Sufferings of United States Officers and Soldiers while Prisoners of War in the Hands of the Rebel Authorities. Being the report of a Commission of Inquiry, appointed by the United States Sanitary Commission*, 19, 95. This 306-page document was initiated after the delivery to the Union of extremely ill and emaciated prisoners from Belle Isle in mid-1864. The clear purpose of the investigation was to place blame on the Confederacy and to excuse any reported poor treatment of Confederate prisoners. While it is interesting and includes a number of firsthand statements, the conclusions should be taken within the purpose of the document.
2. Gillispie, *Andersonvilles of the North*, 29.
3. Cloyd, *Haunted by Atrocity*, 27.
4. Ibid., 44.
5. Ibid., 56-57.

CHAPTER 1: IMPACT OF MODERN WARFARE ON THE HISTORY OF PRISONERS OF WAR
1. Clausewitz, *On War*, 309-311.
2. Spencer, *A Narrative of Andersonville*, 120-121.
3. *Chicago Tribune*, February 14, 1862.
4. Doyle, *Voices from Captivity*, 12-13; and Keller, *The Story of Camp Douglas*, 58-59.
5. Ibid.
6. Ibid.
7. Ibid., 30.
8. Ibid., 12-13.
9. Ibid., 43.
10. Ibid., 16, and Sanders, *Hands of the Enemy*, 21.
11. US War Department, *War of the Rebellion: A Compilation of the Official Records of the Union and Confederate Armies*, Section. II, Vol. III, 157; hereafter referred to as OR, with all references to Series II unless otherwise noted.
12. Ibid., Vol. 1, 560-561.
13. Ibid., 128-129.
14. www.sam.usace.army.mil/Portals/46.
15. www.american-rails.com/beginning.html.
16. www.battlefields.org/learn/srticles/railroads-confrderacy.
17. www.american-rails.com.
18. Hyde, *A Captive of War*, 60-65, 69.
19. Peckenpaugh, *Captives in Blue*, 23.
20. Ferguson, *Life-Struggles Rebel Prisons*, 48, 51.
21. Smedley, *Life in Southern Prisons*, 17-21.

CHAPTER 2: FIVE FACTORS IMPACTING PRISONERS OF THE CIVIL WAR
1. OR, Vol. III, 301.

2. OR, Vol. IV, 13-52, 121. Contained on these pages are a variety of examples of individual exchanges arranged by various officers including Union general George B. McClellan and Confederate general Robert E. Lee. This also included requests from politicians and individual requests from prisoners.

CHAPTER 3: CONDITIONS IN CIVIL WAR PRISONS

1. Sanders, *Hands of the Enemy*, 1.
2. Gillispie, *Andersonvilles of the North*, 66.
3. *Medical and Surgical History of the War of the Rebellion*, Volume 1, Part 111, 30 and 46. There have been no meaningful studies on other factors, such as the Union blockade and availability of medicine, that may have affected recovery at Chimborazo Hospital.
4. Davis, *Andersonville and Other War-Prisons*, 1.
5. US Sanitary Commission, *Narrative of Privations and Sufferings of United States Officers and Soldiers while Prisoners of War in the Hands of the Rebel Authorities*, 69.
6. OR., Vol. III, 47.
7. Spear, *Portals to Hell*, 9-10.
8. McPherson, *Battle Cry of Freedom*, 40, 608, 614.
9. Warner, *Generals in Gray*, xx.
10. Ibid., xviii.
11. Cooper, *In and Out of Confederate Prisons*, Author preface.
12. Burke, *Civil War Journal 1862-1865*.
13. Dufur, *Over the Dead Line or Tracked by Blood-Hounds*, 213.
14. OR, Vol. VI, 434, 461.
15. OR, Vol. VI, 390.
16. OR, Vol VII, 694, 390.
17. Copley, *A Sketch of the Battle of Franklin Tennessee with Reminiscences of Camp Douglas*, 124.
18. Warren, "Diary," 8.
19. Browne, *Four Years in Secessia*, 268.
20. Ibid., 31.
21. Wilson, *A Brief History of the Cruelties and Atrocities of the Rebellion*, 3.
22. Roach, *Prisoner of War, and How Treated*, 61.
23. Ibid., 62.
24. Bagby, *Civil War Diary, 1863-1865*, 9.
25. Spear, *Portals to Hell*, 222.
26. OR, Vol. VI, 132; and Triebe, *Point Lookout Prison Camp and Hospital*, 19.
27. Triebe, *Point Lookout Prison Camp and Hospital*, 20.
28. Allison, *Hell on Belle Isle, Diary of a Civil War POW*, 82.
29. Ibid., 91.
30. Lyon, *In and Out of Andersonville Prison*, 37.
31. Smedley, *Life in Southern Prisons*, 29.
32. Murray, *Immortal Six Hundred*, 59.
33. Ibid., 97.
34. Cooper, *In and Out of Confederate Prisons*, 209.
35. Sprague, *Lights and Shadows in Confederate Prisons*, 51.
36. US Sanitary Commission, *Narrative of Privations and Sufferings of United States Officers and Soldiers while Prisoners of War in the Hands of the Rebel Authorities*, 155.

37. Lyon, *In and Out of Andersonville Prison*, 43.

38. Davis, "Diary," 35.

39. Wyeth, "Cold Cheer at Camp Morton" in *Century Magazine*, XLI, 846-47; and Winslow & Moore, *Camp Morton, 1861-1865*, 108.

40. OR, Vol. VI, 577; and Triebe, *Point Lookout Prison Camp and Hospital*, 33.

41. *Chicago Tribune*, February 22, 1862.

42. Allsion, *Hell on Belle Isle, Diary of a Civil War POW*, 119.

43. Jeffrey, *Richmond Prisons 1861-1862*, 9.

44. Winslow & Moore, *Camp Morton, 1861-1865*, 35.

45. Burke, *Civil War Journal 1862-1865*, January 4, 1864.

46. OR, Vol. VI, 585; and Triebe, *Point Lookout Prison Camp and Hospital*, 31.

47. Cooper, *In and Out of Confederate Prisons*, 56.

48. Peckenpaugh, *Captives in Gray*, 223-225; OR, Vol. VII, 1122, 1279-1283, 1288-1291.

49. *Camp Douglas News*, Summer 2010.

50. OR, Vol. IV, 476.

51. Huff, "Diary," August 1864.

52. Allison, *Hell on Belle Isle, Diary of a Civil War POW*, 82.

53. Ibid., 86.

54. Ibid., 128.

55. Temple, *The Union Prison at Fort Delaware*, 43.

56. Burke, "Civil War Journal," September 26, 1864.

57. Putnam, *A Prisoner of War in Virginia, 1864-65*, 24.

58. Roach, *Prisoner of War, and How Treated*, 58.

59. Hyde, *A Captive Of War*, 108.

60. Murray, "Diary."

61. Hasseltine, *Civil War Prisons*, 67.

62. Cooper, *In and Out of Confederate Prisons*, 218.

63. Davis, "Diary" 36.

64. Kennedy, "Diary," May 7, 1864; and Futch, *History of Andersonville Prison*, revised edition, 32.

65. Peckenpaugh, *Captives in Blue*, 27.

66. Lightcap, *The Horrors of Southern Prisons During the War of the Rebellion*, 38.

67. OR, Vol. VII, 499-500; and Futch, *History of Andersonville Prison*, Revised Edition.

68. OR, Vol VI, 461-464; and Keller, *The Story of Camp Douglas*, 92.

69. OR, Vol. IV, 678-686.

70. Ferguson, *Life-Struggles in Rebel Prisons*, 151.

71. Futch, *History of Andersonville Prison*, revised edition, 97.

72. Trial Record, 4350-4351; and Spencer, *A Narrative of Andersonville*, 223.

73. US Sanitary Commission, *Narrative of Privations and Sufferings of United States Officers and Soldiers while Prisoners of War in the Hands of the Rebel Authorities*, 53.

74. Browne, *Four Years In Secessia*, 322.

75. OR, Vol VI, 575-580.

76. Burke, *Civil War Journal*, March 11, 1864, March 12, 1864, February 14, 1864, September 4, 1864; Bagby, *Civil War Diary 1863-1865*, February 1863, October 1, 1863, November 21, 1864; and Keller, *The Story of Camp Douglas*, 172-178.

77. Burke, *Civil War Journal 1862-1865*, March 11, 1864, March 12, 1864; and Keller, *The Story of Camp Douglas*, 173.

78. Bagby, *Civil War Diary 1863-1865*, November 21, 1864; and Keller, *The Story of Camp Douglas*, 178.

79. Hyde, *A Captive Of War*, 113.

80. Burke, *Civil War Journal*, September 7, 1864.

81. Hyde, *A Captive Of War*, 246.

82. OR, Vol. VII, 954, 1006.

83. Jeffrey, *Richmond Prisons 1861-1862*, 154.

84. Sprague, *Lights and Shadows in Confederate Prisons*, 56.

85. Temple, *The Union Prison at Fort Delaware*, 35, 105.

86. Davidson, *Fourteen Months in Southern Prisons*, 48.

87. Ibid., 95.

88. Ibid., 192.

89. *Ohio State Journal*, September 1, 1863; and Knauss, *Story of Camp Chase*, 136.

90. *Chicago Tribune*, February 19, 1863; and Keller, *The Story of Camp Douglas*, 137.

91. OR, Vol. V, 48, 347, 588, 686; and Keller, *The Story of Camp Douglas*, 137.

92. OR, Vol. VI, 371; and Keller, *The Story of Camp Dougla*, 137.

93. Winslow and Moore, *Camp Morton, 1861-1865*, 29, 91.

94. OR, Vol. V, 6, 487; and Vol. VI, 485.

95. Jeffrey, *Richmond Prisons, 1861-1862*, 111-112.

96. Futch, *History of Andersonville Prison*, Revised Edition, 56; and OR, Vol. VII, 403.

97. Davis, "Diary," 36.

98. Hyde, *A Captive of War*, 128-129.

99. Ibid., 182.

100. Ferguson, *Life-Struggles in Rebel Prisons*, 102.

101. Ibid., 149.

102. Sprague, *Lights and Shadows in Confederate Prisons*, 48.

103. Copley, "Diary," 100-110; and Burke, "Diary," April 3, 1864.

104. Copley, "Diary," 100.

105. Keller, *The Story of Camp Douglas*, 143.

106. Stevenson, *The Southern Side; or, Andersonville Prison*, 155.

107. Copley, *Reminiscences of Camp Douglas*, 136.

108. Hall, *Den of Misery, Indiana's Civil War Prison*, 61.

109. Lightcap, *The Horrors of Southern Prisons During the War of the Rebellion*, 31.

110. Ibid., 34.

111. Cooper, *In and Out of Confederate Prisons*, 58.

112. Keller, *The Story of Camp Douglas*, 109.

113. Trial Report, 2606; and Spencer, *A Narrative of Andersonville*, 202-203.

114. OR, Vol. III, 267.

115. Copley, *Reminiscences of Camp Douglas*, 68-80.

116. Winslow and Moore, *Camp Morton 1861-1865*, 102.

117. Peckenpaugh, *Captives in Gray*, 81.

118. Keller, *The Story of Camp Douglas*, 200.

CHAPTER 4: FACTOR 1

1. OR, Vol. IV, 639.

2. OR, Vol. III, 694; and Peckenpaugh, *Captives in Blue*, 6.

3. Peckenpaugh, *Captives in Blue*, 1.

4. Ibid., 16.

5. OR, Vol. VII, 499-500; and Futch, *History of Andersonville Prison*, Revised Edition, 80.

6. Spencer, *A Narrative of Andersonville*, 18.

7. OR, Vol III, 9.

8. Ibid., 10.

9. Peckenpaugh, *Captives in Gray*, 2.

10. OR, Vol. VI, 30.

11. OR, Vol. III, 236-237.

12. OR, Vol. IV, 618-619, 625-626.

13. OR, Vol. III, 384-385; and Temple, *The Union Prison at Fort Delaware*, 15.

14. OR, Vol III, 301.

15. Sanders, *While in the Hands of the Enemy*, 72.

16. Urban, *Battle Field and Prison Pen or Through the War, and Thrice a Prisoner in Rebel Dungeons*, 85-86.

17. Shepherd, *Narrative of Prison Life At Baltimore and Johnson's Island, Ohio*, 16.

18. OR, Vol. III, 315-16.

CHAPTER 5: FACTOR TWO

1. Sanders, *While in the Hands of the Enemy*, 208.

2. Wilson, *A Brief History of the Cruelties and Atrocities of the Rebellion*, 3.

3. Hyde, *A Captive Of War*, Chapters VIII to XXL, 187.

4. OR, Vol. VI, 558; and Futch, *History of Andersonville Prison*, revised edition, 3.

5. OR, Vol. VIII, 732.

6. Kellogg, *Life and Death in Rebel Prisons*, 131.

7. Lyon, *In and Out Andersonville Prison*, 33.

8. Ferguson, *Life-Struggles in Rebel Prisons*, 82.

9. Roach, *Prisoner of War, and How Treated*, 171.

10. Eby, *Observations of an Illinois Boy in Battle, Camp and Prisons 1861 to 1865*, 199.

11. OR, Vol. IV, 235.

12. Burke, *Civil War Journal*, April 10, 1864 and October 15, 1863; Spear, *Portals of Hell*, 222.

13. Ibid., 7.

14. Ibid., 13-14.

15. OR, Vol. VII, 1092, 1003-1004, 1025, 1042-1043; and Gray, *The Business of Captivity*, 57.

16. Gray, *The Business of Captivity*, 55.

17. OR, Vol. VII, 180-181.

18 OR, Vol. VI, 88.

19. Gray, *The Business of Captivity*, 103.

20. Ibid., Vol VII, 5, 106.

CHAPTER 6: FACTOR THREE

1. OR. Vol. IV, 103.

2. Allison, *Hell on Belle Isle, Diary of a Civil War POW*, 62.

3. Urban, *Battle Field and Prison Pen or Through the War, and Thrice a Prisoner in Rebel Dungeons*, 462.

4. Ferguson, *Life-Struggles in Rebel Prisons*, 79.

5. Glazier, *The Capture, the Prison Pen, and the Escape*, 45.
6. Keller, *The Story of Camp Douglas*, Appendix I and II.
7. Bietzell, *Point Lookout Prison Camp for Confederates*, 181.
8. Winslow and Moore, *Camp Morton, 1861-1865*, 99.
9. OR, Vol. VI, 200.
10. Ibid., 206.
11. OR, Vol. III, 337; Vol. IV, 504; Vol. V, 517; and Peckenpaugh, *Captives in Gray*, 119.
12. OR, Vol. V, 686; and Keller, *The Story of Camp Douglas*, 81.
13. OR, Vol. IV, 407-408, 432; OR, Vol. VII, 954, 1006.
14. Temple, *The Union Prison at Fort Delaware*, 32-38, 88; and Jones, *Civil War Prison Camps*, 29.
15. Keller, *The Story of Camp Douglas*, 93-96.

CHAPTER 7: FACTOR FOUR
1. OR, Vol. IV, 187.
2. Hasseltine, *Civil War Prisons*, 7.
3. Eby, *Observations of an Illinois Boy in Battle, Camp and Prisons 1861 to 1865*, 141-142.
4. Jeffrey, *Richmond Prisons 1861-1862*, 87-88.
5. Putnam, *A Prisoner of War in Virginia, 1864-65*, 66.
6. May 7, 9, 1864 (MS in possession of Charles T. Winship, Atlanta, GA); and Futch, *History of Andersonville Prison*, revised edition, 56.
7. Camp Douglas Restoration Foundation has original documents from Camp Douglas commanders in early 1862 requesting prison guards. Frequently, requests were for three or four guards from a unit. This resulted in guards from several units serving at the same time.
8. OR, Vol. VI, 143-144, 492-493; and Winslow and Moore, *Camp Morton 1861-1895*, 93.
9. Temple, *The Union Prison at Fort Delaware*, 80-81.
10. Gray, *The Business of Captivity*, 19.
11. Triebe, *Point Lookout Prison Camp and Hospital*, 25.
12. Peckenpaugh, *Captives in Gray*, 127.
13. Levy, *To Die in Chicago*, 239.
14. Hasseltine, *Civil War Prisons*, 54.
15. England, *A Short History of the Rock Island Prison Barracks* (Revised Edition), 23.
16. Peckenpaugh, *Captives in Gray*, 81.

CHAPTER 8: FACTOR FIVE
1. Cooper, *In and Out of Confederate Prisons*, 49.
2. Sprague, *Lights and Shadows in Confederate Prisons*, 87-88.
3. Winslow and Moore, *Camp Morton 1861-1865*, 89.
4. For details of Morgan's Raiders at Camp Douglas, see Keller, *The Story of Camp Douglas*.
5. *Camp Douglas News* (Spring 2014). The death rate for Morgan's Raiders is based on the assumption that between 2,000 and 2,500 were incarcerated at the camp, with deaths based on names contained on the monument at Oak Woods Cemetery. Exact figures for the number at the prison and deaths are unknown.
6. For a detailed description of the Raiders see Chapter 5, Futch, *History of Andersonville Prison*, revised edition.
7. Hyde, *A Captive of War*, 228.

8. Hall, *Den of Misery, Indiana's Civil War Prison*, 37.
9. Sherrill, *Soldier's Story*, 11; and Gray, *The Business of Captivity*, 108.
10. Triebe, *Point Lookout Prison Camp and Hospital*, 62.
11. Sprague, *Lights and Shadows in Confederate Prisons*, 50-51.

BIBLIOGRAPHY

BOOKS AND PAPERS

Allison, Don (ed). *Hell on Belle Isle: Diary of a Civil War POW*. Bryan, Ohio: Faded Banner Publications, 1997.

Berry, Thomas F. *Four Years with Morgan and Forest*. Harlow Ratleff Company, 1914, 2017 edition.

Bietzell, Edwin W. *Point Lookout Prison Camp for Confederates*. St. Mary's County Historical Society, 1972.

Camp Douglas News, Camp Douglas Restoration Foundation.

Chemung Historical Journal. Elmira, NY. August 1985.

Chemung Historical Journal. Elmira, NY. August 2002.

Clausewitz, Carl von. *On War*, Vom Kreig, 1832. Anatol Rapoport, ed. Baltimore: Penguin Books, 1968.

Cloyd, Benjamin C. *Haunted by Atrocity: Civil War Prisons in American Memory*. Baton Rouge: Louisiana State University Press, 2010.

Doyle, Robert C. *The Enemy in Our Hands*. Lexington: University Press of Kentucky, 2010.

Doyle, Robert C. *Voices from Captivity*. Lawrence: University Press of Kansas, 1994.

England, Otis Bryan. *A Short History of the Rock Island Prison Barracks*. Revised Edition. History Office US Army Armament, Munitions and Chemical Command, Rock Island, Illinois, 1985.

Futch, Ovid L. *History of Andersonville Prison*, Revised Edition. Gainesville: University Press of Florida, 2011.

Gray, Michael P. *The Business of Captivity: Elmira and Its Civil War Prison*. Kent, OH: Kent State University Press, 2001.

Gillispie, James M. *Andersonvilles of the North: The Myths and Realities of Northern Treatment of Civil War Confederate Prisoners*. Denton, TX: University of North Texas Press, 2008.

Hall, James R. *Den of Misery: Indiana's Civil War Prison*. Gretna, LA: Pelican Press, 2006.

Hasseltine, William B. (ed). *Civil War Prisons*. Kent, OH: Kent State University Press, 1962.

Isham, Asa B., Henry M. Davidson, and Henry B. Furness. *Prisoners of War and Military Prisons, Personal Narratives*. Cincinnati: Lyman and Cushing, 1890.

Jeffrey, William F. *Richmond Prisons, 1861-1862.* Republican Press, 1893.

Karamanski, Theodore J. *Rally 'Round the Flag: Chicago and the Civil War.* New York: Rowman & Littlefield, 2006.

Keller, David L. *Analysis of Five Factors Impacting Confederate Soldiers in Union Prison Camps During the Civil War.* Andersonville National POW Research Program, 2017.

Keller, David L. *Analysis of Five Factors Impacting Union Soldiers in Confederate Prison Camps During the Civil War.* Andersonville National POW Research Program, 2018.

Keller, David L. *The Story of Camp Douglas: Chicago's Forgotten Civil War Prison.* Charleston, SC: History Press, 2015.

Knauss, William H. *Story of Camp Chase.* (1906) Reprint. Columbus, OH: The General's Books, 1990.

Levy, George. *To Die in Chicago: Confederate Prisoners at Camp Douglas 1862-65.* Gretna, LA: Pelican Press, 1999.

McPherson, James M. *Battle Cry of Freedom: The Civil War Era.* New York: Ballantine Books, 1989.

Northrup, John W. *Chronicles from the Diary of a War Prisoner.* Privately Printed, 1904.

Page, James Madison. *The True Story of Andersonville: A Defense of Major Henry Wirz.* Neale Publishing Company, 1908, 2017 edition.

Peckenpaugh, Roger. *Captives in Blue: The Civil War Prisons of the Union.* Tuscaloosa: University of Alabama Press, 2013.

Peckenpaugh, Roger. *Captives in Gray: The Civil War Prisons of the Confederacy.* Tuscaloosa: University of Alabama Press, 2009.

Sanders, Charles W. *While in the Hands of the Enemy: Military Prisons of the Civil War.* Baton Rouge: Louisiana State University Press, 2005.

Spear, Lonnie R. *Portals to Hell: Military Prisons of the Civil War.* Lincoln: University of Nebraska Press, 1997.

Temple, Brian. *Teknion Prison at Fort Delaware.* Jefferson NC: McFarland, 2003.

Triebe, Richard H. *Point Lookout Prison Camp and Hospital: The North's Largest Civil War Prison.* Baltimore: Coastal Books, 2014.

Warner, Ezra J. *Generals in Blue: Lives of the Union Commanders.* Baton Rouge: Louisiana State University Press, 1993.

Warner, Ezra J. *Generals in Gray: Lives of the Confederate Commanders.* Baton Rouge: Louisiana State University Press, 1993.

Winslow, Hattie Lou, and Joseph R. H. Moore. *Camp Morton, 1861-1865*. Indianapolis: Indiana Historical Society, 1940.

DIARIES, JOURNALS, AND LETTERS

Abbot, A. O. *Prison Life in the South 1864-1865*. New York: Harper and Brothers, 1865.

Adams, William Henry. Co. G, 3rd Kentucky Cavalry, CSA. Wartime Letters.

Bagby, Robert Anderson. *Civil War Diary 1863-1865*, transcribed David L. Keller. Camp Douglas Restoration Foundation, 2013.

Boggs, S. S. *Eighteen Months a Prisoner under the Rebel Flag*. Lovington, IL: Privately Printed, 1887.

Brown, William Liston. Civil War Letters. Chicago History Museum.

Browne, Junius Henri. *Four Years in Secessia: Adventures Within And Beyond The Union Lines; Embracing A Great Variety of Facts, Incidents, And Romance of the War*. Hartford, CT: O. D. Case and Company, 1865.

Burke, Curtis R. *Civil War Journal, 1862-1865*. (1915). Reprint. Wilmont, Kathryn (ed). Indianapolis: Indiana Historical Society, 2007.

Burke, Curtis R. "Civil War Journal 1862-1865." Carlisle, PA: Army Heritage & Education Center, 1915.

Cooper, Alonzo. *In and Out of Confederate Prisons*. Oswego, NY: R. J. Oliphant, 1888.

Copley, John M. *A Sketch of the Battle of Franklin, Tennessee, with Reminiscences of Camp Douglas*. Eugene Von Boeckmann, Printer, 1893.

Davidson, H. M. *Fourteen Months in Southern Prisons*. Milwaukee: Daily Wisconsin Printing House, 1865.

Davis, Creed T. *Prison Diary, April 1865*.

Davis, Jefferson. *Andersonville and Other War-Prisons*. New York: Belford Company, 1890.

Dougherty, Michael. *Prison Diary of Michael Dougherty, Late Co. B, 13th., Pa., Cavalry. While confined in Pemberton, Barrett's, Libby, Andersonville and other Southern Prisons*. Chas. A. Dougherty Printer, 1908.

Dufur, S. M. *Over the Dead Line or Tracked by Blood-Hounds*. Privately published, 1902.

Duganne, A. J. H. *Camps & Prisons, Twenty Months in the Department of the Gulf*. New York: J. P. Robens, 1865.

Eby, Henry H. *Observations of an Illinois Boy in Battle, Camp and Prisons 1861 to 1865*. Privately published, 1910.

Ferguson, Joseph. *Life-Struggles in Rebel Prisons*. James M. Ferguson Publisher, 1866.

Francis, Charlies Lewis. *Narrative of a Private Soldier in the Volunteer Army of the United States*. Brooklyn, NY: William Jenkins and Company, 1879.

Glazier, Willard W. *The Capture, the Prison Pen, and the Escape: Giving a Complete History of Prison Life in the South*. Hartford, CT: H. E. Goodwin, 1869.

Hinds, Thomas. *Tales of War Times*. Watertown, NY: Herald, 1904.

Howard, Percy. *Barbarities of the Rebels*. Self published, 1863.

Huff, William D. "Diary, October 4, 1863–May 4, 1865." Chicago History Museum, MSS Alpha 2 H.

Humphreys, Charles C. *Field, Camp, Hospital, Prison in the Civil War, 1863-1865*. Press of George H. Ellis Co., 1918.

Hyde, Solon. *A Captive Of War*. New York: McClure, Phillips and Co., 1900.

Jeffrey, William H. *Richmond Prisons, 1861-1862*. St. Johnsbury, VT: Republican Press, 1893.

Kellogg, Robert H. *Life and Death in Rebel Prisons*. L. Stebbins, 1866.

Lightcap, William H. *Horrors of Southern Prisons during the War of the Rebellion from 1861 to 1865*. Self published, 1911.

Lyon, W. F. *In and Out of Andersonville Prison*. Detroit: Geo. Harland Co. 1905.

Mackey, James Taswell. "Diary of Lieut. James Taswell Mackey of Maury County in the 48th Regiment Tennessee Infantry 1861-65." Museum of the Confederacy, Richmond, Virginia.

Maile, John L. *Prison Life in Andersonville*. Los Angeles: Grafton Publishing Company, 1912.

Moses, Jefferson. "The memoirs, diary, and life of Private Jefferson Moses, Company G, 93rd Illinois Volunteers," 1911.

Murray, J. Ogden. *Immortal Six Hundred: A Story of Cruelty to Confederate Prisoners of War*. Winchester, VA: Eddy Press, 1905.

Nott, Charles C. *Sketches in Prison Camps*. New York: Anson D. F. Randolph, 1865.

Paul, William R. Letters to Mrs. Winnie Paul, October 28, 1864, January 24, 1865, from William Paul, Co. H, 15th Tenn. Cavalry.

Putnam, George. *A Prisoner of War in Virginia, 1864-65*. New York: G. P. Putnam's Sons, 1914.

Roach, A. C. *Prisoner of War and How Treated*. Indianapolis, IN: Railroad City Publishing, 1865.

Roy, Andrew T. *Recollections of A Prisoner of War*. Second Revised Edition. Columbus, OH: J. L. Trauger Printing Co, 1909.

Sabre, G. E. *Nineteen Months a Prisoner of War*. American News Company, 1865.

Sanderson, James M. *My Record in Rebellion*. New York: W. E. Sibell, Stationer and Printer, 1865.

Shepherd, Henry E. *Narrative of Prison Life at Baltimore and Johnson's Island, Ohio*. Baltimore: Commercial Printing & Stationary Co., 1917.

Sherrill, Miles O. *A Soldier's Story: Prison Life and Other Incidents in the War of 1861–'65*. Privately Published, 1904.

Smedley, Charles. *Life in Southern Prisons*. The Ladies' and Gentlemen's Fulton Aid Society, 1865.

Spencer, Ambrose. *A Narrative of Andersonville*. New York: Harper and Brothers, 1866.

Sprague, Homer B. *Lights and Shadows in Confederate Prisons*. New York: G. P. Putnam's Sons, 1915.

Stevenson, Randolph M. D. *Southern Side or Andersonville Prison*. Baltimore, MD: Turnbull Brothers, 1876.

Sturgis, Thomas. *Prisoners of War, 1861-1865*. New York: G. P. Putman's Sons, 1912.

Taylor Family Correspondence, University of Notre Dame, Letters, 1864.

Urban, John R. *Battlefield and Prison Pen or Through the War, and Thrice a Prisoner in Rebel Dungeons*. Philadelphia: Hubbard Brothers, 1872.

US Sanitary Commission. *Narrative of Privations and Sufferings of United States Officers and Soldiers while Prisoners of War in the Hands of the Rebel Authorities. Being the report of a Commission of Inquiry, appointed by the United States Sanitary Commission*. King & Baird, Printer, 1864. (Contained on *Civil War Prisons*. History & Genealogy Reference Library. 70 Books on CD. Ancestry Found, 2016.)

US War Department. *War of the Rebellion, A Compilation Of the Official Records of the Union and Confederate Armies*. Washington, DC: Government Printing Office, 1894-1899.

Walsh, W. A. *Camp Field and Prison Life*. Southwestern Book and Publishing Co., 1870.

Wells, Leroy. Diary, 1861-1862.

Whitaker, William. *A Part of War and Prison Life*. Allen's Laurel Hill Sutlery.

Williams, Robert Thomas. "Diary, Marches, Skirmishes and Battles of the 4th Regiment, Texas Militia between October 1861 to November 1865," transcribed Connie Ragan Seelke.

Williamson, James J. *Prison Life in the Old Capital.* Privately Published, 1911.

Wilson, Thomas L. *A Brief History of the Cruelties and Atrocities of the Rebellion.* Union Congressional Committee, August 29, 1864.

INTERVIEWS AND CORRESPONDENCE

Barr, Charles. Andersonville National Historic Site.

Beckman, Tim. Camp Morton.

Bemis, Kaleb. Research Coordinator, ASC History Office. Rock Island Prison.

Bush, David. Johnson's Island.

Cosk, John. American Civil War Museum.

Crickenberger, Bob. Friends of Point Lookout.

Doyle, Robert C. Author, *The Enemy in our Hands.*

Eaton, George. Command Historian, AMSAS-HI, Rock Island.

Furry, Bill. Illinois State Historical Society.

Gray, Michael P. Author, *The Business of Captivity, Elmira and its Civil War Prison.*

Gregory, Michael. Elmira.

Hall, James R. Author, *Den of Misery, Indiana's Civil War Prison.*

Heyworth, Kathy. Camp Butler.

Hoffman, Dick. Hilltop Historical Society, Camp Chase.

Hopkins, Jennifer. Park Guide, Andersonville National Historic Site.

Karamanski, Theodore J. Author, *Rally 'Round the Flag: Chicago and the Civil War.*

Levy, George. Author, *To Die in Chicago, Confederate Prisoners at Camp Douglas 1862-65.*

Miller, Jake. Interpreter, Fort Delaware.

Rawls, S. Waite III. President, American Civil War Museum Foundation.

Sanders, Charles W. Author, *While in the Hands of the Enemy: Military Prisons of the Civil War* .

Triebe, Richard H. Point Lookout Prison Camp and Hospital.

Young, Don. Johnson's Island Society.

WEBSITES

American Battlefield Trust. www.battlefields.org/learn/srticles/railroads-confrderacy.

American Rails. www.american-rails.com/beginning.html.

US Army Corp of Engineers. www.sam.usace.army.mil/Portals/46.

ACKNOWLEDGMENTS

This book would not be possible without the valuable research of others and the support of the Andersonville National Site POW Research Program. The program graciously funded research on the topic in 2017 and 2018. The staff, especially Superintendent Charles Sellars, Chief of Interpretation and Resource Management Jody Mays, Ranger Jennifer Hopkins, and Ranger Charles Barr were extremely helpful and supportive of the project.

S. Waite Rawls III, retired president, American Civil War Museum Foundation, and Dan Joyce, executive director, The Civil War Museum, located in Kenosha, WI, provided encouragement to conduct the initial research and were instrumental in any success of the program. The board of directors of the Camp Douglas Restoration Foundation, as ever, covered for me as I spent hours researching and writing. Special encouragement from friends including David Bush, Ron Coddington, Doug Dammann, Mike Grey, Ted Karamanski, George Levy, and Don Young made this project possible. Russell Lewis, executive vice president and chief historian of the Chicago History Museum, who passed away during the drafting of this book, was a special friend and mentor. Russell paid me the highest and unwarranted compliment when he referred to me as "a historian." I'll never forget that day and his many contributions to my work. Also, special thanks to all of the historians who have written and compiled valuable information on Union and Confederate prison camps. There are too many to name here. M. J. Grinstead, my faithful editor and proofreader, again, has done a saintly job in putting up with my impossible writing. She has shown patience beyond description. The following at Westholme Publishing provided outstanding help and guidance in making this book possible: Bruce H. Franklin, publisher, Nate Best, copy editor, Tracy Dungan, cartographer, and Trudi Gershenov, cover designer.

Last, but certainly not least, thanks to my understanding wife, Linda, and my ever-present companion Frieda, our fourteen-year-old German shorthaired pointer who passed away shortly after the manuscript was completed.

INDEX